The Epic Book of Mythology

Gods and Creatures

Ethan J Howard

A Blind Guy's View

CONTENTS

Dedicated to my uncle, Matt. You always encouraged me to use my imagination as a child, and without imagination this book would not have been possible.

Much Love.

PREFACE

Dear Readers,

Welcome to "The Epic Book of Mythology: Gods and Creatures." This book is born from my lifelong passion for myths and legends, and my desire to share these enchanting stories with both young and adult audiences. My goal is simple yet profound: to spark the imagination of children and provide a rich source of information for adults.

In crafting this book, I wanted to create something that transcends the typical reading experience. Every page is printed using premium ink and paper, ensuring that the vibrant colors and intricate details of each illustration are brought to life with stunning clarity. This book is designed to be more than just a read; it is a beautiful coffee table piece, a conversation starter in a waiting room, and a cherished addition to any collection.

The digital paintings within these pages capture the essence and wonder of 90 deities and creatures from various mythologies around the world. Each piece was meticulously crafted with a Renaissance impressionistic style in mind, blending historical artistry with modern techniques to create timeless images that evoke awe and inspiration.

I invite you to explore these mythic worlds, to appreciate the artistry, and to let your imagination soar. May this book bring you as much joy and fascination as it brought me in its creation.

Please enjoy and cherish this journey through mythology.

Warmest regards,

Ethan J. Howard

Acknowledgements

First and foremost, I would like to extend my deepest gratitude to Nikkaya Delgado, John Delgado, Sapphire Delgado, Eileen M., Matthew Gray, and Boone Gray. Your meticulous eye for detail, dedication, and relentless desire to ensure every word, every passage, and every nuance was just right have truly made *The Epic Book of Mythology* what it is today. This book is as polished as it is because of your invaluable efforts, and I cannot thank you enough for your incredible work.

To my family and friends, thank you for your unwavering love and support throughout this journey. Your encouragement has been my guiding light, pushing me forward through the challenges and celebrating each triumph along the way. This book exists because of the foundation you've given me, and I am forever grateful.

And to my two children, Hadley and Holden, thank you for allowing "Daddy" the time to sit and work on this book. I hope one day you will enjoy it as much as I have enjoyed creating it.

Thank you all from the bottom of my heart.

1

ACHILLES

(GREEK)

Description

Achilles is one of the most renowned heroes in Greek mythology, known for his exceptional strength, courage, and martial prowess. He is often depicted as a young and handsome warrior, clad in shining armor and wielding formidable weapons. His most distinctive feature is his invulnerability, with the exception of his heel, which became known as his only weak spot.

Origin

Achilles was the son of Peleus, the king of the Myrmidons, and Thetis, a sea nymph. His origin story is steeped in divine intervention and prophecy. According to myth, Thetis attempted to make Achilles immortal by dipping him in the River Styx, holding him by his heel, which remained untouched by the waters and thus vulnerable.

Lore

Achilles is a central figure in Greek mythology, celebrated for his unmatched strength and martial prowess. Born to the sea-nymph Thetis and the mortal king Peleus, Achilles was dipped by his mother into the River Styx, making him invulnerable except for the heel by which she held him—a detail that would later prove to be his downfall. His heroic deeds, fierce temper, and eventual tragic death, caused by an arrow to his heel, have made him a symbol of both the glory and the fleeting nature of life. Achilles' story is immortalized in Homer's

Additional Facts

- **Achilles' Heel**: The term "Achilles' heel" originates from Achilles' singular point of vulnerability and is commonly used to describe a person's principal weakness.
- **Achilles in Art**: Achilles has been a popular subject in classical and modern art, appearing in countless paintings, sculptures, and literary works.
- **The Myrmidons**: The warriors commanded by Achilles were known as the Myrmidons, a group of elite soldiers said to be as loyal as ants, which is reflected in their name deriving from the Greek word for ant.
- **Achilles in Popular Culture**: Achilles' legend has been adapted in various films, books, and television series, including the 2004 film "Troy," where he was portrayed by Brad Pitt.
- **Achilles' Armor**: His armor was considered incredibly powerful and was famously worn by Patroclus before his death, and after Achilles' death, it became a point of contention between Ajax and Odysseus.

Resources

1. "The Iliad" by Homer.

2

AMATERASU

(JAPANESE)

Description

Amaterasu, also known as Amaterasu Ōmikami, is the Japanese sun goddess and one of the principal deities in Shinto religion. She is often depicted as a radiant and beautiful figure, embodying the light and life giving power of the sun. Amaterasu is revered for her role in overseeing the celestial realm and ensuring the vitality of the natural world.

Origin

Amaterasu was born from the left eye of the god Izanagi during the purification ritual he performed after escaping the underworld. Her emergence was accompanied by a dazzling light, signifying her role as the sun goddess. She is considered the progenitor of the Japanese imperial family, with the emperors of Japan believed to be her direct descendants.

Lore

Amaterasu's most famous myth involves her retreat into the Heavenly Rock Cave (Ama no Iwato) following a quarrel with her brother Susanoo, the storm god. Susanoo's reckless behavior and desecration of her sacred spaces drove Amaterasu to hide, plunging the world into darkness. The other gods devised a plan to coax her out by performing a lively dance and placing a mirror outside the cave. Intrigued by the commotion and her reflection, Amaterasu emerged, restoring light to the world. This event underscores her importance in maintaining order and harmony.

Additional Facts

- **The Mirror**: The Yata no Kagami, one of the three Imperial Regalia of Japan, is believed to be the sacred mirror used to lure Amaterasu from the cave. It symbolizes wisdom and honesty.
- **Amaterasu in Festivals**: The Grand Shrine of Ise (Ise Jingu), dedicated to Amaterasu, is one of Japan's most significant and sacred Shinto shrines. The annual festivals held there celebrate her divine presence and blessings.
- **Symbolism**: As the sun goddess, Amaterasu represents life, growth, and renewal. Her presence is essential for the balance of nature and the prosperity of the world.
- **Imperial Lineage**: The Japanese emperor is considered the "son of the sun" due to Amaterasu's status as the mythological ancestor of the imperial family, reinforcing the divine right to rule.

Resources

1. "Records of Ancient Matters" by Kojiki.
2. "Chronicles of Japan" by Shoki Nihon.

3

ANANSI

(WEST AFRICA)

Description

Anansi is a prominent figure in West African folklore, particularly among the Akan people of Ghana. He is often depicted as a spider but can also appear as a man or a combination of both. Known as the trickster god, Anansi is celebrated for his cunning, wit, and cleverness, often using his intelligence to outsmart others.

Origin

Anansi's tales originate from the oral traditions of the Ashanti people of Ghana and have spread throughout West Africa. His stories were carried to the Caribbean and Americas by enslaved Africans, where they evolved and integrated into local folklore, becoming an essential part of African diaspora cultures.

Lore

Anansi's lore is vast and varied, consisting of numerous stories where he uses his cleverness to achieve his goals, often at the expense of other, larger animals or even gods. One famous tale involves Anansi tricking the sky god Nyame to obtain all the world's stories. Anansi's adventures often carry moral lessons, teaching values such as wisdom, humility, and the importance of intelligence over brute strength.

Additional Facts

- **Anansi Stories**: Known as "Anansesem" in the Akan language, these stories were traditionally told by elders around fires and have been passed down through generations.
- **Cultural Influence**: Anansi's tales have influenced folklore in the Caribbean and the Southern United States, leading to similar characters like Br'er Rabbit.
- **Anansi in Literature**: Anansi appears in numerous works of literature, including Neil Gaiman's "Anansi Boys," where he is portrayed as the father of two sons who inherit his trickster traits.
- **Anansi Festivals**: Some communities in Ghana and the Caribbean celebrate Anansi with festivals that include storytelling, music, and dance to honor his role in their cultural heritage.
- **Anansi the Teacher**: Despite his trickster nature, Anansi is often seen as a teacher, imparting wisdom through his actions and the consequences that follow, thus serving as an educational figure.

Resources

1. "A Treasury of African Folklore" by Herold Courlander.
2. "African Folktales: Traditional Stories of the Black World" by Roger Abrahams.

4

ANUBIS

(EGYPTIAN)

Description

Anubis, also known as Anpu, is one of the most iconic deities in ancient Egyptian mythology. He is typically depicted as a man with the head of a jackal or as a full jackal. Anubis is associated with mummification and the afterlife, guiding souls to the underworld and protecting the deceased.

Origin

Anubis is believed to be the son of Osiris, the god of the afterlife, and Nephthys, the goddess of mourning. In some myths, he is also considered the son of Set, the god of chaos. Anubis' role as the god of mummification and protector of graves predates the rise of Osiris in the Egyptian pantheon.

Lore

Anubis played a crucial role in Egyptian funerary rites. He was responsible for embalming the dead and presiding over the mummification process, ensuring that the deceased's body was properly prepared for the afterlife. Anubis also guided souls through the underworld, weighing their hearts against the feather of Ma'at, the goddess of truth and justice, to determine their fate. This process, known as the "Weighing of the Heart," was pivotal in deciding whether a soul would enter the afterlife or be devoured by the monster Ammit.

Additional Facts

- **Jackal Symbolism**: Anubis' jackal form is linked to his role as a protector of graves. Jackals were often seen around cemeteries, and Anubis was believed to ward off grave robbers and evil spirits.
- **Anubis in Art**: Anubis is frequently depicted in ancient Egyptian tombs and temples, reflecting his importance in the funerary practices. Statues and amulets of Anubis were common burial items to invoke his protection.
- **Cult Center**: The primary cult center for Anubis was in Cynopolis (the "City of the Dog"), where he was venerated as the city's patron deity.
- **The Name Anubis**: The Greek name "Anubis" is derived from the Egyptian "Inpu" or "Anpu," which means "decay" or "royal child."

Resources:

1. "The Egyptian Book of the Dead"
2. "The Complete Gods and Goddesses of Ancient Egypt" by Richard Wilkinson.

5

APHRODITE

(GREEK)

Description

Aphrodite is the Greek goddess of love, beauty, and desire. Often depicted as an extraordinarily beautiful woman, she embodies the ideal of physical attractiveness and sensuality. She is frequently shown with flowing golden hair and radiant, enchanting features that captivate all who behold her.

Origin

Aphrodite's origins are unique among the Greek gods. According to Hesiod's "Theogony," she was born from the sea foam when the severed genitals of Uranus were cast into the sea by his son Cronus. Another tradition, detailed in Homer's "Iliad," identifies her as the daughter of Zeus and Dione. Regardless of her birth story, she emerged from the sea fully formed and was immediately recognized for her divine beauty.

Lore

Aphrodite played a crucial role in many myths and stories, often involving themes of love and attraction. One of her most famous tales is the judgment of Paris, where she was awarded the golden apple marked "For the Fairest," leading to the Trojan War. Aphrodite was married to Hephaestus, the god of blacksmiths, but she had numerous lovers, including Ares, the god of war. Her affairs and interventions often had significant consequences in mythological narratives, highlighting her influence and power over gods and mortals alike.

Additional Facts

- **Symbols:** Aphrodite is often associated with symbols of beauty and love, such as the rose, dove, swan, and myrtle.Aphrodite in Art:** She has been a popular subject in art for centuries, inspiring countless sculptures, paintings, and literary works. One of the most famous depictions is the statue "Venus de Milo," which resides in the Louvre Museum.
- **Aphrodite's Temples**: The most significant temple dedicated to Aphrodite was in Paphos, Cyprus, which was considered her birthplace and a major center of her worship.
- **Aphrodite's Children**: Among her many children are Eros (Cupid), the god of love, and Aeneas, a hero of Troy who played a crucial role in Roman mythology.
- **Aphrodite in Popular Culture**: Aphrodite continues to be a symbol of beauty and love in modern culture, appearing in literature, movies, and video games, where she is often portrayed as a powerful and alluring deity.

Resources

1. "The Iliad" by Homer
2. "Theogony" by Hesiod.

6

ARES

(Greek)

Description

Ares is the Greek god of war, known for his fierce and aggressive nature. He is often depicted as a handsome yet violent and intimidating figure, clad in armor and carrying weapons such as a spear and shield. Unlike other deities associated with strategic aspects of war, Ares represents the brutal and chaotic nature of battle.

Origin

Ares is the son of Zeus, the king of the gods, and Hera, the queen of the gods. Despite his powerful lineage, Ares was not widely revered in Greek culture due to his association with the destructive and tumultuous aspects of warfare. His Roman counterpart is Mars, who was held in higher regard in Roman mythology.

Lore

Ares features prominently in many Greek myths, often portraying him as a destabilizing force. In the "Iliad," Ares sides with the Trojans during the Trojan War, showcasing his penchant for conflict. His numerous love affairs, especially with Aphrodite, the goddess of love, are well-documented. Their affair produced several children, including Phobos (fear) and Deimos (terror), who often accompanied Ares into battle.

One notable myth involving Ares is his capture by the Aloadae giants, Otus and Ephialtes, who trapped him in a bronze jar for a year until Hermes, the messenger god, rescued him. This story highlights his vulnerability and contrasts with his warlike nature.

Additional Facts

- **Ares and Aphrodite**: Despite his violent nature, Ares had a passionate and adulterous relationship with Aphrodite. Their love story is a prominent theme in both Greek mythology and art.
- **Ares in Modern Culture**: Ares continues to appear in modern literature, movies, and video games, often embodying the destructive power of war. He is a character in various DC Comics and was portrayed by David Thewlis in the 2017 film "Wonder Woman."

Resources

1. "The Iliad" by Homer
2. "Theogony" by Hesiod.

7

ARTEMIS

(GREEK)

Description

Artemis is the Greek goddess of the hunt, wilderness, moon, and chastity. She is often depicted as a youthful and athletic maiden, dressed in a short tunic suitable for hunting, with a bow and quiver of arrows. Artemis exudes a sense of independence and strength, embodying the spirit of untamed nature.

Origin

Artemis is the daughter of Zeus, the king of the gods, and Leto, a Titaness. She is the twin sister of Apollo, the god of the sun and music. According to myth, Artemis was born on the island of Delos and assisted in the birth of her brother, which established her as a protector of childbirth and young children.

Lore

Artemis is a prominent figure in many Greek myths, known for her fierce protectiveness of her virginity and her followers. One famous myth is the story of Actaeon, a hunter who stumbled upon Artemis bathing. As punishment for his transgression, Artemis transformed him into a stag, and he was subsequently torn apart by his own hunting dogs.

Artemis is also known for her role in the tale of Orion, a giant huntsman. Depending on the version of the myth, Orion was either a hunting companion or a lover of Artemis. In some versions, he was killed either by Artemis herself, in a fit of anger, or by Apollo, who was jealous of their relationship.

Additional Facts

- **Symbols**: Artemis is often associated with the moon, deer, hunting dogs, and cypress trees. The silver bow and arrow are her primary symbols.
- **irgin Goddess:** As one of the three virgin goddesses of Olympus, alongside Athena and Hestia, Artemis valued her chastity and fiercely protected it.
- **Artemis in Modern Culture**: Artemis continues to appear in modern literature, movies, and video games. She is often portrayed as a symbol of feminine strength and independence. Notable appearances include Rick Riordan's "Percy Jackson & the Olympians" series.

Resources:

1. "The Iliad" by Homer

8

ATHENA

(Greek)

Description

Athena is the Greek goddess of wisdom, warfare, and crafts. She is often depicted as a majestic and serene figure, clad in armor and a helmet, carrying a shield and spear. Athena is usually accompanied by an owl, symbolizing wisdom, and the olive tree, representing peace and prosperity. Unlike Ares, who represents the chaotic and brutal aspects of war, Athena embodies strategic warfare and intellectual prowess.

Origin

Athena is the daughter of Zeus, the king of the gods, and Metis, a Titaness. According to myth, Zeus swallowed Metis while she was pregnant with Athena because of a prophecy that her child would be more powerful than its father. Later, Zeus experienced a severe headache, and Hephaestus, the blacksmith god, split Zeus's head open with an axe, from which Athena emerged fully grown and clad in armor. Her birth from Zeus's head symbolizes her association with intellect and rationality.

Lore

Athena plays a vital role in numerous Greek myths and epic tales. She is known for her wisdom and guidance to heroes like Odysseus, whom she aided during his long journey home in Homer's "Odyssey." Athena was also a key figure in the "Iliad," supporting the Greeks during the Trojan War and providing strategic counsel.

One famous myth involves Athena's contest with Poseidon over the patronage of Athens. Poseidon offered the city a saltwater spring by striking his trident, while Athena provided an olive tree, symbolizing peace and prosperity. The citizens chose Athena's gift, and the city was named after her.

Additional Facts

- **Symbols**: Athena is commonly associated with the owl, the olive tree, the Aegis (a protective cloak or shield), and the Gorgoneion (a head of Medusa used as a protective amulet).
- **Athena Parthenos**: One of the most famous statues of Athena was the colossal Athena Parthenos, created by the sculptor Phidias, which stood in the Parthenon in Athens.
- **Virgin Goddess**: Athena is one of the three virgin goddesses of Olympus, along with Artemis and Hestia. She is known for her chastity and independence.

Resources

1. "The Iliad" by Homer

9

BALDUR

(NORSE)

Description

Baldur, also spelled Baldr or Balder, is one of the most beloved and significant gods in Norse mythology. Known as the god of light, purity, and beauty, Baldur is often described as radiantly handsome, kind, and just. He is the son of Odin, the chief of the gods, and Frigg, the goddess of love and fertility. Baldur's home is called Breidablik, a place so pure that nothing impure can exist there.

Origin

Baldur's origin lies in the rich tapestry of Norse mythology, which is primarily recorded in the Poetic Edda and the Prose Edda, collections of ancient Norse poems and stories. These texts were written down in the 13th century but are based on much older oral traditions. Baldur's tales are central to the mythology, symbolizing themes of life, death, and rebirth.

Lore

One of the most famous stories about Baldur is his death, which is a pivotal event in Norse mythology. Baldur began having dreams of his own death, which troubled the gods greatly. His mother, Frigg, sought to protect him by making everything in the world vow never to harm him. However, she overlooked the mistletoe, considering it too insignificant to be a threat.

Loki, the trickster god, discovered this oversight and crafted a dart from mistletoe. During a game where the gods amused themselves by throwing harmless objects at Baldur, Loki handed the dart to the blind god Höðr and guided his hand to throw it. The dart struck Baldur, killing him instantly. This event caused immense grief among the gods and set off a chain of events leading to Ragnarok, the end of the world in Norse mythology.

Additional Facts

- **Resurrection and Symbolism:** Baldur's death and his expected return after Ragnarok symbolize the cycles of life, death, and rebirth. He is seen as a Christ-like figure in Norse mythology, embodying themes of sacrifice and hope.
- **Protection:** Before his death, Baldur was considered invulnerable due to his mother's efforts to protect him. His vulnerability to mistletoe highlights the theme of fate and destiny in Norse myth.
- **Literary References:** Baldur appears in various Norse sagas and poems, including the Poetic Edda and the Prose Edda. He is also referenced in modern literature, such as J.R.R. Tolkien's works and Neil Gaiman's "Norse Mythology."

Resources

1. "The Prose Edda" by Snorri Sturluson: A key source of Norse mythology, containing many tales of the gods, including Baldur.
2. "The Poetic Edda" translated by Carolyne Larrington: A collection of Old Norse poems that provide insight into the myths and legends of the Norse gods.

10

BANSHEE

(CELTIC)

Description

A banshee, known as "bean sí" in Irish, is a supernatural being from Irish folklore, often depicted as a female spirit who wails or shrieks to foretell the death of a family member. Banshees are typically described as having a gaunt and eerie appearance, with long, flowing hair and a deathly pallor. They can appear as a beautiful young woman, a matronly figure, or a terrifying old hag, depending on the lore. Regardless of their form, they are always shrouded in mystery and sorrow.

Origin

The legend of the banshee originates from Irish mythology and has been a part of Celtic culture for centuries. The term "banshee" is derived from the Irish "bean sídhe," meaning "woman of the fairy mound" or "fairy woman." In Celtic mythology, fairies and spirits were believed to inhabit ancient burial mounds known as "síde" or "sídhe." The banshee is closely associated with these otherworldly realms and is considered a messenger from the spirit world.

Lore

Banshees are believed to be harbingers of death, their mournful cries serving as an omen that someone in the household is about to die. According to legend, the banshee does not cause death but rather warns of its impending arrival. The wail of a banshee is described as a chilling, mournful sound that can be heard from great distances, often in the dead of night. It is said that the closer the banshee's cry, the more imminent the death.

In some traditions, banshees are considered protective spirits who watch over families, particularly those of noble lineage. Each family was believed to have its own banshee, who would appear to mourn the death of a family member. This aspect of the banshee underscores her role as a guardian and mourner rather than a malevolent force.

Additional Facts

- **Appearance Variations:** Banshees can appear in different forms, from a youthful maiden with flowing hair to a decrepit old hag. These variations may reflect different aspects of death and mourning.
- **Cultural Significance:** The banshee is an enduring symbol in Irish culture, representing the intersection between the living and the spirit world. Her wail is both a warning and a sign of respect for the deceased.

Resources

1. "Fairy and Folk Tales of the Irish Peasantry" by W.B. Yeats: A collection of Irish folklore that includes stories of banshees.
2. "The Banshee: The Irish Death Messenger" by Patricia Lysaght: A comprehensive study of the banshee legend and its cultural significance.

11

BASILISK

(European)

Description

The Basilisk is a legendary creature often described as the "king of serpents." It typically features a blend of characteristics from various animals: the head and legs of a rooster, complete with a comb and wattles, a long, serpentine body covered in scales, and in some depictions, the Basilisk has wings similar to a dragon, adding to its fearsome appearance.

Origin

The myth of the Basilisk originates from ancient Greek and Roman literature. The name "Basilisk" comes from the Greek word "basiliskos," meaning "little king," reflecting its supposed regal and deadly nature. Pliny the Elder, a Roman naturalist, described the Basilisk in his work "Natural History" as a small serpent with a deadly gaze and venomous breath.

Lore

The Basilisk as a legendary serpent or reptilian creature is often referred to as the "King of Serpents." Known for its deadly powers, the Basilisk can kill with just a glance, as its gaze is said to be lethal to any living being. In some tales, its breath is toxic, with the ability to wither plants, poison water, and kill anything in its path. The Basilisk's weakness is often described as its own reflection or the crowing of a rooster, which can cause its death. This creature is a symbol of untamed power, feared across many ancient legends.

Additional Facts

- **Harry Potter:** The Basilisk gained modern fame through J.K. Rowling's "Harry Potter" series, where it is featured in "Harry Potter and the Chamber of Secrets" as a giant serpent.
- **Medieval Bestiaries**: In medieval bestiaries, the Basilisk was often used as a moral symbol, representing the consequences of sin and evil.
- **Multiple Depictions**: Throughout history, the Basilisk has been depicted in various forms, from a giant serpent to a creature with the body of a rooster and the tail of a serpent.

Resources

1. "Natural History" by Pliny the Elder
2. "Basilisk" on Encyclopedia Britannica
3. "The Book of Beasts: Being a Translation from a Latin Bestiary of the Twelfth Century" by T.H. White

12

BASTET

(Egyptian)

Description

Bastet is an ancient Egyptian goddess associated with home, fertility, and childbirth, as well as war and protection. She is typically depicted as a lioness or as a woman with the head of a lioness or a domestic cat. Bastet embodies both nurturing and fierce qualities, reflecting her dual role as a protective deity and a warrior goddess.

Origin

Bastet originated in the Nile Delta region of ancient Egypt, specifically in the city of Bubastis, where she was venerated as the local deity. Over time, her worship spread throughout Egypt. Initially, she was depicted as a lioness, symbolizing her role as a warrior goddess, but later, her image softened to that of a domestic cat, reflecting her nurturing aspects. Bastet is the daughter of Ra, the sun god, and often associated with the Eye of Ra, embodying his protective and vengeful aspects.

Lore

Bastet's lore is rich with stories that emphasize her protective and nurturing qualities. She was revered as a guardian of the home, warding off evil spirits and disease, particularly those affecting women and children. As the goddess of fertility and childbirth, she was invoked to bless mothers and their children with health and safety. In her lioness form, Bastet was a fierce warrior goddess, defending the pharaoh and the nation while upholding Ma'at (order and justice). One notable myth recounts her battle against the serpent Apep, the embodiment of chaos, highlighting her role as a protector of Ra, the sun god, and the world order.

Additional Facts

- **Cat Worship**: Cats were highly revered in ancient Egypt due to their association with Bastet. Killing a cat, even accidentally, was considered a grave offense punishable by death.
- **Dual Nature**: Bastet's dual nature as both a nurturing mother figure and a fierce warrior is symbolized by her transformation from a lioness to a domestic cat over time.
- **Symbols**: Bastet is often depicted with symbols such as the sistrum (a musical instrument), which she used to drive away evil spirits, and a basket, representing fertility and abundance.

Resources

1. "The Complete Gods and Goddesses of Ancient Egypt" by Richard Wilkinson.
2. "Egyptian Mythology: A Guide to the Gods, Goddesses, and Traditions of Ancient Egypt" by Geraldine Pinch.

13

CENTAUR

(GREEK)

Description

A centaur is a mythical creature with the upper body of a human and the lower body of a horse. Originating from Greek mythology, centaurs are often depicted as wild and unruly beings, embodying a duality of human intelligence and animalistic instinct. They are commonly associated with untamed nature and are seen both as noble warriors and as hedonistic revelers.

Origin

The concept of centaurs first emerged in ancient Greek mythology. According to myth, centaurs are the offspring of Ixion, a king punished by Zeus, and Nephele, a cloud made in the image of Hera. The union of Ixion and Nephele produced the first centaurs, who then populated the regions of Thessaly and Arcadia. Centaurs are prominently featured in various Greek myths, representing the blend of human and animalistic traits.

Lore

Centaurs appear in numerous myths and legends, often highlighting themes of duality, conflict, and wisdom:

- **Chiron the Wise**: One of the most famous centaurs is Chiron, known for his wisdom, kindness, and knowledge of medicine and healing. Unlike other centaurs, Chiron was civilized and educated, serving as a mentor to many Greek heroes, including Achilles, Asclepius, and Hercules. His teachings and guidance helped shape these heroes' destinies.

- **The Battle with the Lapiths**: A significant myth involving centaurs is their battle with the Lapiths, a neighboring tribe. At the wedding of Pirithous, the king of the Lapiths, the centaurs became drunk and attempted to abduct the bride and other women. This led to a violent conflict, symbolizing the struggle between civilization and barbarism.

Additional Facts

- **Symbolism of Duality**: Centaurs embody the dual nature of humanity, combining the rational mind of a human with the untamed instincts of a horse. This duality symbolizes the internal conflict between reason and passion.

- **Cultural Variations**: While centaurs are primarily associated with Greek mythology, similar hybrid creatures appear in other cultures. For example, the Indian mythology includes Kinnaras, celestial beings with human and horse part.

Resources

1. "The Iliad" and "The Odyssey" by Homer: Epic poems that include references to centaurs and their interactions with Greek heroes.

2. "Metamorphoses" by Ovid: Contains various myths involving centaurs, including their battle with the Lapiths and the story of Chiron.

14

CERBERUS

(GREEK)

Description

Cerberus is the formidable, multi-headed hound from Greek mythology known for guarding the entrance to the Underworld. Traditionally depicted as having three heads, Cerberus is often shown with a serpent's tail, a mane of snakes, and lion-like claws. Each head of Cerberus represents the past, present, and future, or in some interpretations, birth, youth, and old age.

Origin

Cerberus is one of the many monstrous offspring of Typhon and Echidna, making him a sibling to other notorious creatures such as the Hydra, Chimera, and Orthrus. Typhon and Echidna, known for their fearsome and destructive nature, passed these traits onto their progeny, with Cerberus becoming one of the most recognizable figures in Greek mythology.

Lore

Cerberus's most notable role is as the watchdog of Hades, the Greek god of the Underworld. In many myths, he is an invincible and fearsome creature. One of the most famous stories involving Cerberus is the twelfth labor of Hercules, in which the hero is tasked with capturing Cerberus and bringing him to the surface world.

Additional Facts

- **Appearance:** While often depicted with three heads, some versions of the myth describe Cerberus as having as many as fifty or a hundred heads.
- **Symbolism:** Cerberus represents the boundary between life and death, embodying the fear of death and the unknown.
- **Mythical Encounters:** In addition to Hercules, Cerberus was also encountered by Orpheus, who charmed him with music, and Aeneas, who drugged him with a honeycake.

Resources

1. "The Iliad" and "The Odyssey" by Homer: These epic poems include references to the Underworld and its guardian, Cerberus.
2. "The Library of Greek Mythology" by Apollodorus**:** Offers detailed accounts of Cerberus's origins and his role in various myths.
3. "The Aeneid" by Virgil**:** Provides a Roman perspective on Greek myths. "...Encounter with the Cerberus"

15

CHIMERA

(GREEK)

Description

The Chimera is a monstrous creature from Greek mythology, known for its composite form and terrifying appearance. It is typically depicted as having the body and head of a lion, a goat's head rising from its back, and a serpent or dragon as its tail. Sometimes, the lion's head is described as breathing fire, adding to its fearsome nature.

Origin

The Chimera is the offspring of the monsters Typhon and Echidna, making it a sibling to other fearsome creatures like Cerberus, the Hydra, and the Sphinx. Typhon and Echidna, both formidable in their own right, were considered among the most dangerous beings in Greek mythology, and their progeny carried on their legacy of terror.

Lore

The most famous tale involving the Chimera is its battle with the hero Bellerophon. Sent by King Iobates of Lycia on a seemingly impossible quest to kill the Chimera, Bellerophon was aided by the winged horse Pegasus, which he tamed with the help of the goddess Athena. Riding Pegasus, Bellerophon attacked the Chimera from the air, using his spear to avoid the creature's deadly breath and ultimately slaying it.

The Chimera's myth underscores themes of bravery and ingenuity, as Bellerophon had to overcome not just the physical might of the beast but also its supernatural attributes. This story highlights the hero's clever use of Pegasus and divine assistance to achieve victory.

Additional Facts

- **Symbol of Hybrid Monsters:** The Chimera's composite form has made it a symbol of hybrid monsters in literature and art. The term "chimera" is now used metaphorically to describe any mythical or fictional creature with parts taken from various animals.
- **Fire-Breathing Legend:** The Chimera is one of the earliest examples in mythology of a fire-breathing creature, a trait that has been echoed in various legends and fantasy stories involving dragons and other mythical beasts.
- **Genetic Term:** In modern science, the term "chimera" is used in genetics to describe an organism containing cells from two different zygotes, reflecting the mythological creature's mixed nature.

Resources

1. "The Iliad" by Homer: Contains references to the Chimera, providing context within the broader tapestry of Greek mythology.
2. "The Library of Greek Mythology" by Apollodorus: A comprehensive source for many Greek myths, including the story of Bellerophon and the Chimera.

16

CÚ CHULAINN

(Irish)

Description

Cú Chulainn, a legendary hero from Irish mythology, is renowned for his exceptional strength, bravery, and warrior skills. Often depicted as a handsome, youthful warrior with an imposing presence, he is sometimes shown wielding his famed spear, Gáe Bolg. His defining features include his striking appearance during the ríastrad, or battle frenzy, where his body contorts and his appearance becomes fearsome and otherworldly.

Origin

Cú Chulainn was originally named Sétanta. He was born to Deichtine, the sister of King Conchobar mac Nessa of Ulster, and the god Lugh, giving him both mortal and divine heritage. His supernatural lineage endowed him with extraordinary abilities from a young age.

Lore

Cú Chulainn earned his name as a child when he killed the guard dog of the smith Culann in self-defense and offered to take its place until a new one could be raised, becoming known as the "Hound of Culann." He trained under the warrior woman Scáthach, mastering combat and receiving the deadly spear, Gáe Bolg. In the epic

(The Cattle Raid of Cooley), Cú Chulainn defends Ulster single-handedly against Queen Medb's forces, showcasing his heroic prowess. Mortally wounded in battle, he ties himself to a standing stone to die on his feet, cementing his legacy as a symbol of bravery.

Additional Facts

- **Battle Frenzy (Ríastrad)**: When in battle frenzy, Cú Chulainn's body would contort and transform, making him nearly invincible and utterly terrifying to his enemies.
- **Scáthach's Training**: Cú Chulainn was one of the few who survived and completed training under Scáthach, which included overcoming numerous life-threatening challenges.
- **Loyal Hound**: The name Cú Chulainn reflects his loyalty and commitment, symbolizing his readiness to protect and serve his people even at great personal cost.
- **Defensive Feat: In the "Táin Bó Cúailnge,"**: Cú Chulainn used ingenious strategies like single combat challenges to slow down Queen Medb's advancing forces, showcasing not just his strength but his intellect.

Resources

1. "The Táin" translated by Thomas Kinsella:** A comprehensive translation of the epic "Táin Bó Cúailnge," detailing Cú Chulainn's exploits.

17

CUPID

(GREEK)

Description

Cupid, known as Eros in Greek mythology, is the god of love, desire, and affection. He is often depicted as a winged, cherubic boy with a bow and arrow, which he uses to ignite love and desire in his targets. In some representations, Cupid appears as a handsome, youthful figure, emphasizing his role in stirring romantic and erotic feelings.

Origin

Cupid is the Roman counterpart of the Greek god Eros. In Roman mythology, he is the son of Venus (Aphrodite in Greek mythology), the goddess of love, and Mars (Ares in Greek mythology), the god of war. In earlier Greek myths, Eros was a primordial deity, one of the first beings to emerge from Chaos, embodying the fundamental force of attraction that brought the world into existence.

Lore

Cupid's stories often revolve around his mischievous nature and the consequences of his arrows. One of the most famous myths involving Cupid is his romance with Psyche:

- **Cupid and Psyche**: Psyche was a mortal princess of extraordinary beauty, which aroused Venus's jealousy. Venus commanded Cupid to make Psyche fall in love with the most despicable man. However, Cupid himself fell in love with her. He visited Psyche every night in complete darkness, forbidding her to look at him. Psyche, urged by her jealous sisters, eventually lit a lamp to see her lover and discovered Cupid's divine identity. Feeling betrayed, Cupid left her. Psyche endured numerous trials set by Venus to win back Cupid's love. Ultimately, Psyche's perseverance and love triumphed, and she was granted immortality to live with Cupid forever.

Additional Facts

- **Dual Nature**: Cupid's arrows come in two types—golden-tipped arrows that cause uncontrollable love and lead-tipped arrows that incite aversion and hatred.
- **Symbols of Love**: Cupid's imagery with a bow and arrow has become synonymous with love and Valentine's Day, representing the sudden, unpredictable nature of love.

Resources

1. "Metamorphoses" by Ovid: A primary source that includes the tale of Cupid and Psyche and other myths involving Cupid.
2. "The Golden Ass" by Apuleius: Contains the detailed and famous story of Cupid and Psyche.

18

CYCLOPS

(GREEK)

Description

Cyclopes (plural of Cyclops) are giant beings from Greek mythology, characterized by their single, round eye in the middle of their forehead. They are known for their immense strength and often depicted as primitive and brutish, yet some Cyclopes possess significant skills, particularly in blacksmithing.

Origin

The Cyclopes' origins vary in Greek mythology. There are generally two distinct groups:

1. **The Elder Cyclopes**: These are the three primordial Cyclopes—Brontes (Thunder), Steropes (Lightning), and Arges (Bright). They are the sons of Uranus (Sky) and Gaia (Earth). These Cyclopes were skilled blacksmiths who forged Zeus's thunderbolts, Poseidon's trident, and Hades's helm of darkness.

2. **The Younger Cyclopes**: These are the Cyclopes encountered by Odysseus in Homer's "Odyssey," most notably Polyphemus. These Cyclopes are depicted as more savage and less cultured than their elder counterparts. They are usually considered the offspring of Poseidon and a nymph.

Lore

The Elder Cyclopes were instrumental in the Greek gods' victory over the Titans. Imprisoned by their father Uranus and later by Cronus, they were freed by Zeus during the Titanomachy. In gratitude, they provided the gods with powerful weapons.

Polyphemus, the most famous of the Younger Cyclopes, appears in Homer's "Odyssey." Odysseus and his men become trapped in Polyphemus's cave. The Cyclops begins to eat the men, prompting Odysseus to devise a plan. They blind Polyphemus with a heated stake, and Odysseus cunningly escapes by hiding under the sheep in Polyphemus's flock.

Additional Facts

- **Master Craftsmen**: The Elder Cyclopes were renowned for their metalwork. They created some of the most powerful weapons and tools in Greek mythology, including Zeus's thunderbolts.

- **Symbolism**: The single eye of the Cyclops symbolizes a focused vision but also a limited perspective, often leading to their downfall due to a lack of depth perception and foresight.

Resources

1. "The Odyssey" by Homer: A primary source for the tale of Polyphemus and his encounter with Odysseus.

19

DIANA

(ROMAN)

Description

Diana is the Roman goddess of the hunt, the moon, and nature, often associated with wild animals and woodland. She is typically depicted as a youthful and beautiful maiden, dressed in a short tunic suitable for hunting, and often accompanied by a bow and arrows. Diana is also associated with the crescent moon, sometimes shown wearing a crescent diadem.

Origin

Diana's origins are rooted in Roman mythology, but she shares many attributes with the Greek goddess Artemis, who was also a virgin huntress and moon goddess. Diana is the daughter of Jupiter (Zeus in Greek mythology) and Latona (Leto). She has a twin brother, Apollo, who is associated with the sun.

Lore

Diana's myths often emphasize her independence, chastity, and connection to nature:

- **The Birth of Diana and Apollo**: Diana and her twin brother Apollo were born on the island of Delos. Their mother, Latona, sought refuge there to give birth after being pursued by the jealous Hera (Juno in Roman mythology).
- **Actaeon**: One of the most famous myths involving Diana is the story of Actaeon. Actaeon, a hunter, accidentally stumbled upon Diana while she was bathing. As punishment for seeing her naked, Diana transformed him into a stag, and he was subsequently hunted down and killed by his own hounds.

Additional Facts

- **Triple Goddess**: Diana is often part of a triple goddess aspect, where she is associated with Hecate and Selene. Diana represents the hunt and the wilderness, Hecate the underworld and magic, and Selene the moon.
- **Sanctuaries**: The most famous sanctuary dedicated to Diana is the Temple of Diana at Ephesus, one of the Seven Wonders of the Ancient World.

Resources

1. "Metamorphoses" by Ovid: Contains several myths involving Diana, including the stories of Actaeon and Niobe.
2. "The Aeneid" by Virgil: Features mentions of Diana and her influence in Roman culture.

20

DRAGON (WYVERN)

(European and Chinese)

Description

Dragons are mythical creatures often depicted as large, serpent-like beings with formidable powers. They typically have scales, wings, sharp claws, and the ability to breathe fire or emit other elemental forces such as ice or poison. While their appearance and abilities can vary widely across different cultures, dragons are universally recognized as symbols of power, wisdom, and, sometimes, malevolence.

Origin

The concept of dragons appears in the mythologies and folklore of many cultures around the world:

- **European Dragons**: In Western traditions, dragons are often portrayed as evil and destructive, hoarding treasures and being defeated by heroic knights. These dragons are typically depicted with large, bat-like wings and the ability to breathe fire.
- **Chinese Dragons**: In Eastern traditions, particularly in China, dragons are considered benevolent creatures associated with water, rain, and agriculture. Chinese dragons are often shown as long, snake-like beings with four legs, no wings, and whiskers on their faces. They symbolize strength, power, and good fortune.

Lore

Dragons play various roles in myths and legends, reflecting their cultural significance:

- **St. George and the Dragon**: One of the most famous Western dragon tales involves St. George, who rescues a princess from a dragon and slays the beast, symbolizing the triumph of good over evil.
- **The Dragon and the Pearl**: In Chinese mythology, dragons are often depicted chasing a flaming pearl, which represents wisdom and enlightenment. The dragon's pursuit of the pearl symbolizes the quest for knowledge and truth.

Additional Facts

- **Guardians and Hoarders**: In many myths, dragons are depicted as guardians of treasure, symbolizing both the wealth and the danger inherent in seeking it.
- **Elemental Powers**: Depending on the culture, dragons can control various elements like fire, water, air, or earth, reflecting their immense power and versatility.

Resources

1. "Firedrake: A Dragon Mythology Anthology" edited by Cherith Baldry: A collection of dragon myths from various cultures.

21

DRYAD

(GREEK)

Description

Dryads are ethereal beings often depicted as beautiful, graceful women who are deeply connected to trees and forests. They possess features that reflect the essence of nature, such as long, flowing hair that resembles leaves or vines, skin with a natural, earthy hue, and eyes that mirror the colors of the woodland. Some dryads may exhibit bark-like patterns on their skin, and their hair might change color with the seasons. They are known for their enchanting beauty and serene presence.

Origin

The concept of dryads originates from ancient Greek mythology. The word "dryad" comes from the Greek word "drys," meaning "oak." Originally, dryads were specifically associated with oak trees, but over time, the term has come to encompass all tree nymphs. Dryads are considered to be the daughters of Zeus and Gaia, the primordial deities representing the sky and the earth. These nature spirits were believed to inhabit and protect the trees and forests, living symbiotically with their arboreal homes.

Lore

In Greek mythology, dryads are often portrayed as shy and reclusive beings who prefer to stay hidden within their forests. They are intrinsically tied to their respective trees, and their lives are directly linked to the well-being of these trees. If a dryad's tree were to die, the dryad would also perish. This connection underscores their role as guardians of the forest, fiercely protective of their natural domain. Many myths depict dryads as benevolent spirits who assist those who respect nature but can become vengeful if their homes are threatened.

One of the most famous myths involving a dryad is the story of Daphne, who was transformed into a laurel tree to escape the pursuit of Apollo. This tale highlights the deep connection between dryads and their trees, as well as their desire for freedom and protection.

Additional Facts

- **Tree Meld:** Dryads have the ability to merge with their trees, becoming invisible to the naked eye. They can emerge from their trees at will, making them elusive and difficult to spot.
- **Healing Touch:** Dryads possess the power to heal plants, animals, and even humans using their connection to nature's life force. This healing ability is often depicted as a gentle, glowing touch that revitalizes life.
- **Elemental Manipulation:** Dryads can control aspects of the natural environment, such as summoning vines, manipulating roots, or calling forth gentle breezes. This power enables them to protect their forests and aid those in need.

Resources

1. "The Greek Myths" by Robert Graves: A comprehensive collection of Greek myths, including stories about dryads and other nature spirits.

22

DWARF

(GERMANIC, NORSE)

Description

Dwarves, also known as "dvergar" in Old Norse, are mythical beings commonly found in various European mythologies, most notably in Norse mythology. These beings are typically characterized by their short stature, immense strength, and exceptional skills in craftsmanship, mining, and metalworking. Dwarves are often depicted as rugged and resilient, with long beards and a deep connection to the earth.

Origin

The concept of dwarves originates from early Germanic and Norse mythology. According to Norse cosmology, dwarves were created from the maggots that consumed the flesh of the primordial giant Ymir. These maggots were transformed by the gods into intelligent beings who dwelled in the earth and stone. They are often associated with the underground realms, where they mine precious metals and forge powerful artifacts.

Lore

Dwarves are renowned for their skills as blacksmiths and craftsmen. In many myths, they are credited with creating some of the most powerful and magical items in the world. For instance, in Norse mythology, they forged Thor's hammer, Mjölnir, Odin's spear, Gungnir, and the magical ring Draupnir. Dwarves are also known for their craftsmanship in jewelry and other metalworks, often depicted as the creators of beautiful and enchanted items.

Despite their small size, dwarves are formidable warriors. They are fiercely protective of their treasures and homes, often residing in deep, labyrinthine caves filled with gold and precious gems. Dwarves are depicted as stubborn and sometimes grumpy, but they are also known for their loyalty and bravery.

Additional Facts

- **Types of Dwarves:** In various mythologies, there are different types of dwarves. For example, in Norse mythology, there are the dark elves or "dökkálfar," who are sometimes conflated with dwarves. In other traditions, dwarves are divided into different clans or families, each with its own unique traits and skills.
- **Role in Mythology:** Dwarves often serve as secondary characters in myths, aiding gods and heroes with their unparalleled craftsmanship. They are also featured in stories where their cunning and resourcefulness play a crucial role in overcoming challenges.

Resources

1. "The Prose Edda" by Snorri Sturluson: A collection of Norse myths that includes stories about the creation of dwarves and their role in the mythology.
2. "The Poetic Edda" translated by Carolyne Larrington: Another important source of Norse mythology, featuring poems that mention dwarves and their exploits.

23

ELF

(Germanic, Scandinavian, Celtic)

Description

Elves are mythical beings often depicted as elegant, otherworldly creatures with pointed ears, sharp features, and a timeless beauty. They are typically portrayed as tall and slender, with keen senses and an affinity for nature. Elves possess an ethereal grace and agility, moving with a fluidity and poise that surpasses that of humans. Their eyes, often described as bright and expressive, reflect their deep wisdom and longevity.

Origin

The concept of elves originates from Germanic, Scandinavian, and Celtic folklore. In these early traditions, elves were considered nature spirits or demigods, living in forests, meadows, and other natural settings. The Old English word "ælf" and the Old Norse "álfr" refer to these supernatural beings. Over time, elves evolved in literature and myth, becoming integral to the fantasy genre, most notably through the works of J.R.R. Tolkien in his Middle-earth legendarium.

Lore

Elves are often depicted as immortal or extremely long-lived, with lifespans extending into centuries or millennia. They are known for their wisdom, knowledge, and magical abilities. Elves typically live in harmony with nature, residing in majestic forests or mystical realms hidden from human eyes. They are skilled in archery, swordsmanship, and various forms of magic, and are often portrayed as protectors of the natural world.

In many myths and stories, elves are divided into different subraces or factions, each with unique characteristics and cultures. For example, in Tolkien's lore, there are the High Elves (Noldor), Wood Elves (Silvan Elves), and Sea Elves (Teleri), each with their own distinct societies and histories. Elves are also known for their craftsmanship, creating exquisite weapons, jewelry, and artifacts imbued with magical properties.

Additional Facts

- **Weaknesses:** While elves are formidable in many aspects, they often have vulnerabilities tied to their mystical nature. For example, they may be susceptible to certain magical curses or bound by ancient oaths and prophecies.
- **Cultural Significance:** Elves have been a part of European folklore for centuries, influencing various cultural traditions and celebrations. In some Scandinavian folklore, elves are associated with the land and its fertility, often honored during seasonal festivals.
- **Literary References:** Elves have been a central theme in numerous works of fiction. Besides Tolkien's "The Lord of the Rings" and "The Hobbit," they appear in the works of authors like C.S. Lewis, Andrzej Sapkowski (The Witcher series), and many others.
- **Modern Interpretations:** In contemporary fantasy literature, films, and games, elves are often depicted as noble, wise, and sometimes aloof beings. They are featured in popular series such as "The Elder Scrolls," "Warcraft," and "Dungeons & Dragons."

Resources

1. "The Lord of the Rings" by J.R.R. Tolkien: A seminal work in modern fantasy literature, featuring richly developed elven characters and lore.
2. "The Silmarillion" by J.R.R. Tolkien: Explores the deep history of Middle-earth, including the creation and history of the elves.

24

FAIRY (SPRITE, PIXIE)

(EUROPEAN)

Description

Fairies are mythical beings found in folklore around the world, particularly in European traditions. They are often depicted as small, winged creatures with magical powers, though their appearance, size, and nature can vary greatly across different cultures. Fairies are known for their enchanting beauty, mischief, and connection to nature.

Origin

The concept of fairies originate in Celtic mythology, and medieval folklore. They are often linked to the spirits of nature, ancestors, or ancient deities. In Celtic mythology, fairies are part of the "Otherworld," a realm inhabited by supernatural beings. The term "fairy" itself is derived from the Old French word "faerie," which refers to enchantment and magical beings.

Lore

Types of Fairies: Fairies can take many forms, including:

- **Pixies**: Small, mischievous fairies often associated with the West Country of England.
- **Elves**: Typically depicted as taller, more human-like beings, often associated with Norse and Germanic mythology.
- **Brownies**: Helpful household fairies found in Scottish and English folklore, known for performing chores at night in exchange for small offerings.
- **Will-o'-the-Wisps**: Mysterious lights that lead travelers astray, often associated with swampy areas.

Additional Facts

- **Symbolism of Nature**: Fairies often symbolize the natural world and its mysteries. They are guardians of nature, associated with plants, animals, and the changing seasons.
- **Fairy Beliefs Around the World**: While most commonly associated with European folklore, similar beings exist in cultures worldwide, such as the jinn in Arabic folklore, the nymphs in Greek mythology, and the kami in Japanese Shinto.

Resources

1. **"The Fairy-Faith in Celtic Countries" by W.Y. Evans-Wentz**: Explores the historical and cultural significance of fairies in Celtic folklore.

25

FAUN (SATYR)

(ROMAN, GREEK)

Description

Fauns are creatures from Roman mythology, characterized by their half-human, half-goat appearance. They have the upper body of a human, complete with arms and a torso, and the lower body of a goat, including legs, hooves, and often a small tail. Fauns typically have pointed ears, curly hair, and sometimes small horns on their heads. They are known for their playful, carefree, and mischievous nature.

Origin

Fauns are the Roman counterparts of the Greek satyrs, both of which are associated with the god of wine, revelry, and nature—Bacchus (Dionysus in Greek mythology). The fauns are considered to be the offspring or companions of Faunus, the Roman god of the forest, plains, and fields, who himself is a nature deity associated with the fertility of the land and the vitality of the wild.

Lore

Fauns play a significant role in Roman and Greek mythology, often depicted as companions of Bacchus/Dionysus, engaging in dancing, music, and revelry. Their association with nature and the rustic countryside also links them to pastoral life and the wilderness.

- **Pan and the Satyrs**: The Greek god Pan, who shares similarities with fauns and satyrs, is a rustic deity of shepherds and flocks. He is often depicted playing the panpipes, an instrument closely associated with these creatures.
- **Dancing and Music**: Fauns are frequently shown dancing and playing musical instruments like flutes and panpipes. Their music is believed to have the power to enchant and mesmerize both humans and animals.

Additional Facts

- **Dual Nature**: Fauns embody the duality of human and animal characteristics, symbolizing the balance between civilization and the wild, reason and instinct.
- **Symbolism**: They are often seen as symbols of fertility, nature, and the untamed wilderness, representing the primal forces of life.

Resources

1. "The Metamorphoses" by Ovid: Contains references to fauns and satyrs within various mythological narratives.
2. "The Greek Myths" by Robert Graves: Provides detailed accounts of Greek mythology, including the stories of Pan and the satyrs, which are closely related to fauns.

26

FENRIR

(NORSE)

Description

Fenrir is a monstrous wolf from Norse mythology, known for his immense size and strength. Often depicted as a gigantic and fearsome wolf with dark fur and glowing eyes, Fenrir embodies chaos and destruction. His boundless power and menacing appearance make him one of the most terrifying figures in Norse legends.

Origin

Fenrir is one of the offspring of the trickster god Loki and the giantess Angrboda. He has two siblings, the serpent Jormungandr and the half-dead, half-living Hel. The gods of Asgard, aware of the prophecy that Fenrir would bring about great destruction, sought to control him from a young age.

Lore

The gods' fear of Fenrir's potential led them to take drastic measures to bind him. Initially, they tried to restrain him with regular chains, but Fenrir broke them effortlessly. Finally, they commissioned the dwarves to forge Gleipnir, a magical and unbreakable ribbon made from six impossible ingredients: the sound of a cat's footfall, the beard of a woman, the roots of a mountain, the breath of a fish, the sinews of a bear, and the spittle of a bird.

To trick Fenrir into being bound by Gleipnir, the gods challenged him to test his strength against it. Sensing a trap, Fenrir agreed only if one of the gods placed their hand in his mouth as a pledge of good faith. The brave god Tyr volunteered, and when Fenrir found himself unable to break free from Gleipnir, he bit off Tyr's hand in rage.

Fenrir remained bound until the prophesied events of Ragnarök, the end of the world. During Ragnarök, Fenrir would break free and join forces with the giants against the gods. He would ultimately kill Odin, the Allfather, in a brutal battle before being slain by Odin's son Vidar.

Additional Facts

- **Symbol of Destruction:** Fenrir represents ultimate destruction and chaos in Norse mythology, symbolizing the uncontrollable forces that can bring about the end of the world.
- **Tyr's Sacrifice:** The god Tyr's willingness to sacrifice his hand highlights themes of bravery and the necessity of personal sacrifice for the greater good.

Resources

1. "The Poetic Edda" translated by Carolyne Larrington: A primary source of Norse myths, including references to Fenrir and his role in Ragnarök.
2. "The Prose Edda" by Snorri Sturluson: Another essential source that provides detailed accounts of Fenrir.

27

FRIGG

(NORSE)

Description

Frigg, also known as Frigga, is one of the most important goddesses in Norse mythology. She is the wife of Odin, the chief of the gods, and the mother of Baldur, the beloved god of light. Frigg is revered as the goddess of love, marriage, fertility, and fate. She is often depicted as a wise and protective figure, embodying the qualities of motherhood and womanhood. Frigg's primary abode is Fensalir, a splendid hall in Asgard, the realm of the gods.

Origin

Frigg's origins are deeply rooted in Germanic and Norse mythology. Her name is derived from the Old Norse "frigg" and the Old High German "frīja," both meaning "beloved" or "to love." As the chief goddess of the Aesir, the principal pantheon in Norse mythology, Frigg's stories and attributes have been passed down through the Poetic Edda and the Prose Edda, collections of Old Norse poems and prose compiled in the 13th century from earlier traditional sources.

Lore

Frigg is best known for her wisdom and foreknowledge. Unlike Odin, who actively seeks out knowledge, Frigg is believed to possess an inherent understanding of fate and destiny, yet she rarely reveals what she knows. One of the most poignant myths involving Frigg is the story of her son Baldur's death. Foreseeing his demise, Frigg extracted promises from all things in the world not to harm Baldur, but she overlooked the mistletoe, thinking it harmless. Loki, the trickster god, exploited this oversight, leading to Baldur's tragic death. This event underscores Frigg's deep maternal love and her sorrow, as well as her association with fate.

Frigg is also associated with domestic affairs and the protection of families. She is often invoked by women for blessings related to marriage, childbirth, and household matters. Her role as a mother and protector highlights her nurturing and caring nature.

Additional Facts

- **Attributes:** Frigg is often depicted with symbols of domesticity and fertility, such as keys, spindles, and mistletoe. She is sometimes shown weaving clouds, a reference to her control over the sky and weather.
- **Literary References:** Frigg appears in several key Norse texts, including the Poetic Edda and the Prose Edda. She is also referenced in modern adaptations of Norse mythology, such as the works of J.R.R. Tolkien and Neil Gaiman.
- **Modern Interpretations:** Frigg continues to be a significant figure in contemporary media, including literature, television, and video games. She is often portrayed as a powerful and wise matriarch, embodying the values of love and loyalty.

Resources

1. "The Prose Edda" by Snorri Sturluson: Provides detailed accounts of Norse myths, including stories of Frigg.

28

GANESHA

(HINDU)

Description

Ganesha, also known as Ganapati or Vinayaka, is one of the most revered deities in Hinduism. He is easily recognizable by his elephant head, large ears, and a pot-bellied human body. Ganesha is often depicted with four arms, holding various objects such as a goad, a noose, a modak (sweet), and a broken tusk. His vahana (vehicle) is a mouse or rat, symbolizing humility and the ability to overcome obstacles.

Origin

Ganesha's origins are deeply rooted in Hindu mythology. He is the son of Parvati and Shiva, two principal deities in the Hindu pantheon. There are several myths regarding Ganesha's birth. One popular story recounts how Parvati created Ganesha from the turmeric paste used for her bath and set him to guard her door while she bathed. When Shiva returned and was denied entry by Ganesha, he became enraged and decapitated the boy. Parvati, distraught, demanded Shiva to restore her son. Shiva replaced Ganesha's head with that of an elephant, bringing him back to life.

Lore

Ganesha is known as the remover of obstacles and the god of beginnings, intellect, and wisdom. He is worshipped at the start of rituals and new ventures to ensure success and the smooth running of activities. His large elephant head symbolizes wisdom and understanding, while his big ears signify that he listens to the prayers of his devotees.

One well-known myth involves Ganesha's competition with his brother, Kartikeya. They were tasked with racing around the world. While Kartikeya set off on his peacock, Ganesha circled his parents, declaring that they represented the entire universe. This act demonstrated his wisdom and devotion, earning him the victory.

Additional Facts

- **Elephant Head Symbolism**: Ganesha's elephant head symbolizes immense wisdom and understanding. His large ears indicate his ability to listen to his devotees.
- **The Broken Tusk**: One of Ganesha's tusks is broken, representing the idea of sacrifice and that wisdom often comes with loss. According to myth, he broke it off to use as a pen to write the epic Mahabharata.

Resources

1. "Mythologies of the World: The Illustrated Guide to Mythical Creatures and Their Origins" by Tony Allan: "Ganesha".

29

GENIE (DJINN)

(ARABIAN)

Description

Genies, also known as jinn or djinn, are supernatural beings that feature prominently in Middle Eastern, Islamic, and Arabian folklore. Often depicted as powerful entities capable of granting wishes, genies can be either benevolent or malevolent. They are traditionally depicted as spirits made of smokeless fire, possessing magical abilities and the power to shape-shift.

Origin

The concept of genies originates from pre-Islamic Arabian religion and mythology, but they are most famously known from Islamic texts. In Islamic theology, jinn are mentioned in the Quran as beings created from smokeless fire, existing in a parallel world to humans. They have free will and can choose to do good or evil.

Lore

Genies are often associated with magical lamps or bottles, a concept popularized by stories such as "Aladdin and the Magic Lamp" from the collection "One Thousand and One Nights" (also known as "The Arabian Nights"). According to these tales, releasing a genie from its lamp grants the releaser a number of wishes. However, dealing with genies can be tricky, as their interpretation of wishes can be literal and sometimes mischievous.

In folklore, genies live in a variety of places, including abandoned buildings, ruins, deserts, and bodies of water. They are believed to have their own societies, complete with kings, tribes, and social structures. Some tales describe genies as guardians of hidden treasures, while others portray them as tempters leading humans astray.

Additional Facts

- **Types of Genies:** There are different types of jinn, including Marid (often depicted as the most powerful), Ifrit (known for their strength and often malevolent nature), and Ghoul (cannibalistic and shape-shifting jinn).
- **Islamic Belief:** In Islam, jinn are considered real beings that coexist with humans. They are held accountable for their actions and will be judged on the Day of Judgment. Some jinn are believed to be capable of possessing humans, which has led to various rituals and practices intended to protect against or exorcise jinn.

Resources

1. "One Thousand and One Nights" translated by Richard Francis Burton: A classic collection of Middle Eastern and South Asian stories, featuring several tales about jinn.
2. "Jinn and Genies: A Journey Through Islamic History" by Amira El-Zein: A comprehensive study on the historical and cultural significance of jinn in Islamic tradition.

30

GIANT

(GREEK, NORSE)

Description

Giants are mythological beings characterized by their enormous size and great strength. They appear in the folklore and mythology of various cultures around the world, often depicted as towering, human-like figures with immense power. While their appearance and nature can vary, giants are typically portrayed as formidable and often fearsome creatures.

Origin

The concept of giants has roots in many ancient mythologies, where they often represent the primal forces of nature, chaos, and the unknown. Some prominent examples include:

- **Greek Mythology**: In Greek mythology, giants, or Gigantes, were born from Gaia (Earth) and Uranus (Sky). They are best known for their role in the Gigantomachy, a great battle against the Olympian gods.
- **Norse Mythology**: Known as Jotnar, Norse giants are primordial beings who dwell in Jotunheim, one of the Nine Realms. They are often in opposition to the gods of Asgard, led by Odin.

Lore

Giants feature prominently in various mythological stories, often as antagonists or embodiments of natural forces:

- **Greek Gigantomachy**: The Gigantomachy was a fierce battle between the giants and the Olympian gods. The giants, seeking to overthrow the gods, were ultimately defeated with the help of Heracles.
- **Norse Jotnar**: In Norse mythology, the Jotnar frequently clash with the Aesir gods. Notable giants include Ymir, the primordial giant from whose body the world was created, and Loki, who, though often associated with the gods, is of giant descent.

Additional Facts

- **Symbolism**: Giants often symbolize the untamed and chaotic forces of nature, representing obstacles that heroes must overcome.
- **Cultural Variations:** Different cultures have unique interpretations of giants. For instance, in Celtic mythology, giants are often depicted as ancestral figures, while in Hindu mythology, the Rakshasas are giant demons who oppose the gods.

Resources

1. "Giants, Monsters, and Dragons: An Encyclopedia of Folklore, Legend, and Myth" by Carol Rose: "Giants".

31

GNOME

(EUROPEAN)

Description

Gnomes are mythical creatures often depicted as small, humanoid beings with a deep connection to the earth. Typically portrayed with a beard, wearing a pointed hat and simple, rustic clothing, gnomes are known for their industrious nature, wisdom, and affinity for nature and underground environments. They are often seen as guardians of hidden treasures and the natural world.

Origin

The concept of gnomes can be traced back to Renaissance magic and alchemy. The term "gnome" was first introduced by the Swiss alchemist Paracelsus in the 16th century, who described them as earth elementals, beings that live underground and have a deep connection to the earth. Over time, gnomes became a staple of European folklore, particularly in Germanic and Scandinavian traditions.

Lore

Gnomes feature prominently in various myths and stories, often highlighting their roles as guardians, craftsmen, and nature spirits:

- **Guardians of Treasure**: Gnomes are frequently depicted as protectors of buried treasures and valuable minerals. They are believed to have the ability to move through the earth effortlessly, a trait that allows them to hide and safeguard riches from greedy humans.
- **Master Craftsmen**: Known for their exceptional skills in craftsmanship, gnomes are often credited with creating exquisite items, such as jewelry, tools, and magical artifacts. Their expertise in metallurgy and woodworking is unparalleled.

Additional Facts

- **Symbolism of Earth**: Gnomes are strongly associated with the element of earth, symbolizing stability, endurance, and the hidden treasures of the natural world.
- **Variations in Folklore**: Different cultures have their own versions of gnomes, such as the "Tomte" in Scandinavian folklore, a small, bearded figure who protects farms and homes, especially during the winter.
- **Gnome Kings and Realms**: Some stories depict gnomes as having their own kings and subterranean realms, where they live in harmony with nature and other mystical beings.

Resources

1. "The Complete Fairy Tales of the Brothers Grimm": Contains several stories featuring gnomes and other mythical creatures.

32

GOBLIN

(EUROPEAN)

Description

A goblin is a small, grotesque creature known for its mischievous and malevolent nature. They are often depicted with green or gray skin, sharp teeth, and pointy ears. Their appearances vary widely across different cultures, but they typically have exaggerated, twisted features and a cunning, malevolent expression. Goblins are known for their love of trouble, often engaging in pranks and devious activities. They are nocturnal beings, preferring dark, hidden places such as caves, forests, or underground lairs.

Origin

The concept of goblins originates from European folklore, particularly from medieval and early modern periods. The term "goblin" is believed to have derived from the Greek word "kobalos," meaning "rogue" or "knave." Goblins have been a staple in the mythologies of various cultures, including British, Germanic, and Scandinavian traditions. They are often considered a type of fairy or demon, inhabiting the same mystical realms as elves, dwarves, and other supernatural beings.

Lore

In folklore, goblins are portrayed as troublesome creatures who delight in causing chaos and discomfort. They are known for their love of mischief, ranging from harmless pranks to more sinister deeds such as stealing livestock or abducting children. Goblins have a knack for finding treasure, often hoarding shiny objects and gold in their lairs.

One popular tale is the story of the "Goblin King," a powerful and cunning leader who rules over a tribe of goblins. This character has been popularized in various literary and cinematic works, most notably in J.R.R. Tolkien's "The Hobbit" and the film "Labyrinth," where David Bowie famously portrayed the Goblin King.

Additional Facts

- **Weaknesses:** Goblins are often depicted as being weak to sunlight, iron, and certain magical protections. These vulnerabilities make them cautious and elusive, preferring to strike under cover of darkness.
- **Trickery and Cunning:** Goblins are renowned for their cleverness and ability to deceive. They use their wits to outsmart humans and other creatures, often setting traps or using illusions to achieve their goals.
- **Craftsmanship:** Despite their malevolent nature, goblins are sometimes credited with exceptional craftsmanship, particularly in forging weapons and creating traps. This skill is often attributed to their need for survival in harsh environments.

Resources

1. "The Hobbit" by J.R.R. Tolkien: Features goblins as antagonists in Bilbo Baggins' adventure through Middle-earth.

33

GREMLIN

(EUROPEAN)

Description

Gremlins are mythical creatures often depicted as mischievous and mechanically inclined entities, known for causing malfunctions in machinery and technology. These creatures are typically small, impish, and possess a mischievous demeanor. Their physical appearance can vary, but they are often illustrated with exaggerated features, sharp teeth, and a mischievous grin.

Origin

The concept of gremlins is relatively modern, originating in the early 20th century, particularly during the early years of aviation. The term "gremlin" was popularized by British Royal Air Force (RAF) pilots during World War II, who blamed these mythical creatures for unexplained mechanical issues and failures in their aircraft. The word itself is believed to be derived from the Old English word "gremian," which means "to vex."

Lore

The lore of gremlins primarily revolves around their propensity to cause trouble, especially in mechanical and technological contexts:

1. **Aviation and Military**: During World War II, RAF pilots often spoke of gremlins tampering with their aircraft, causing mysterious malfunctions and accidents. This folklore served both as a way to explain technical difficulties and as a form of dark humor to cope with the dangers of flying.

2. **Folklore and Fiction**: Gremlins have been featured in various works of fiction, most notably in Roald Dahl's book "The Gremlins," published in 1943. Dahl, who was himself an RAF pilot, depicted these creatures as mischievous but ultimately helpful beings who could also aid in mechanical repairs if treated kindly.

Additional Facts

- **Variations**: While gremlins are most commonly associated with aviation, they have also been depicted in various other contexts, including automotive and household appliances.
- **Humor and Folklore**: Gremlins serve as a humorous explanation for technical failures and are a testament to human creativity in attributing mysterious occurrences to mythical beings.

Resources

1. "The Gremlins" by Roald Dahl: This book, written by the famous author, provides an early fictional portrayal of gremlins and their antics.

2. "Gremlins: The Return of the Mischievous Imps" by John C. Wright: A comprehensive guide to little creatures.

34

GRIFFIN

(GREEK)

Description

The griffin is a legendary creature with the body, tail, and back legs of a lion, and the head, wings, and talons of an eagle. This combination symbolizes both terrestrial and aerial prowess, embodying the virtues of strength, courage, and protection. The griffin is often depicted as a majestic and powerful guardian, often associated with guarding treasures and priceless possessions.

Origin

The griffin's origins can be traced back to ancient civilizations, including Mesopotamian, Persian, and Egyptian cultures. The creature is prominently featured in Greek mythology and medieval European heraldry. Its earliest known depictions date back to around 3000 BCE, found in artifacts from ancient Iran and Egypt.

Lore

Griffins play various roles in mythology and folklore, often symbolizing protection and divine power:

- **Greek Mythology**: In Greek mythology, griffins were said to guard the gold deposits in the mountains of Scythia against the one-eyed Arimaspians. They were considered sacred to Apollo, the god of the sun, prophecy, and the arts.
- **Medieval Europe**: In medieval European lore, griffins were depicted as noble creatures that guarded treasure and possessed healing powers. They were often seen in coats of arms and heraldry, symbolizing strength, vigilance, and protection.

Additional Facts

- **Symbol of Duality**: The griffin's combination of lion and eagle attributes symbolizes the duality of power and wisdom, as well as the harmony between the earth and sky.
- **Guardianship**: Griffins are often depicted as guardians of treasures and sacred sites. They are believed to be fierce protectors, attacking anyone who threatens their charge.
- **Healing Powers**: Some legends suggest that griffins possess healing powers, with their feathers and claws used in ancient medicine to treat ailments and wounds.

Resources

1. "Mythical Creatures Bible: The Definitive Guide to Legendary Beings" by Brenda Rosen: Provides an overview of various mythical creatures, including the griffin, and their roles in different cultures.

35

HADES

(GREEK)

Description

Hades is the Greek god of the underworld, the realm of the dead. Often depicted as a stern and regal figure, Hades is usually shown with a dark beard, a crown or helmet (the Helm of Darkness), and holding a bident (a two-pronged staff). His presence is often associated with death and the afterlife, but he is also considered a just and fair ruler of his domain.

Origin

Hades is one of the Olympian gods, born to the Titans Cronus and Rhea. He is the brother of Zeus, Poseidon, Hera, Demeter, and Hestia. After the defeat of the Titans, the world was divided among the three brothers: Zeus received the sky, Poseidon the sea, and Hades the underworld. Despite being one of the major gods, Hades is not considered an Olympian because he resides in the underworld rather than on Mount Olympus.

Lore

Hades is a central figure in many myths, often revolving around themes of death, the afterlife, and the balance of life:

- **Abduction of Persephone**: One of the most well-known myths involving Hades is the abduction of Persephone. Hades fell in love with Persephone, the daughter of Demeter, and took her to the underworld to be his queen. Demeter's grief caused the earth to become barren. To resolve this, Zeus decreed that Persephone would spend part of the year with Hades (autumn and winter) and part with her mother (spring and summer), explaining the seasons.

Hades is also known for the Helm of Darkness, which grants the wearer invisibility. This helm was a key asset during the Titanomachy, the war against the Titans.

Additional Facts

- **Not Evil**: Unlike many modern interpretations, Hades is not considered evil in Greek mythology. He is a stern but fair ruler, overseeing the balance of life and death.
- **Riches and Wealth**: Hades is also associated with wealth, as precious minerals and gems come from beneath the earth. His name is sometimes used as a synonym for wealth and prosperity.
- **Underworld Ruler**: The underworld is divided into various regions, including Tartarus (a deep abyss for the wicked), the Elysian Fields (a paradise for the righteous), and the Asphodel Meadows (for ordinary souls). Hades oversees all these areas.

Resources

1. "The Greek Myths" by Robert Graves: A comprehensive retelling of Greek myths, including those involving Hades.

36

HEKATE

(GREEK)

Description

Hekate, also spelled Hecate, is a goddess in Greek mythology associated with magic, witchcraft, the moon, and crossroads. She is often depicted as a powerful, mysterious figure holding torches, keys, serpents, or a dagger, and sometimes shown with three faces or bodies to symbolize her dominion over earth, sea, and sky. Hekate's imagery is deeply tied to the night and the liminal spaces between the worlds.

Origin

Hekate's origins are somewhat obscure, but she is believed to be a Titaness, the daughter of the Titans Perses and Asteria. Unlike many Titans, Hekate retained her power after the Olympian gods overthrew the Titans, owing to her alignment with the Olympians. She was highly revered and honored by Zeus, who granted her authority over the heavens, earth, and sea.

Lore

Hekate's myths often highlight her role as a goddess of transitions, magic, and the unseen world:

- **The Abduction of Persephone**: Hekate plays a crucial role in the myth of Persephone's abduction by Hades. After Persephone's disappearance, Hekate, carrying torches, helps Demeter search for her daughter. Eventually, Hekate becomes a companion to Persephone in the underworld, further cementing her association with the realms of the dead.
- **The Triple Goddess**: Hekate is often depicted in a triple form, representing her dominion over the past, present, and future, or her ability to see in all directions at crossroads. This triple form also links her to the phases of the moon—waxing, full, and waning.
- **Magic and Witchcraft**: Hekate is considered the goddess of magic and witchcraft, and many ancient sorcerers and witches invoked her in their spells and rituals. She is often associated with herbs, potions, and necromancy.

Additional Facts

- **Symbolism**: Hekate's symbols include torches, keys, serpents, daggers, and the moon. These objects represent her roles in guiding the way, unlocking the mysteries of the unseen, and her connection to the night.
- **Modern Worship**: Hekate remains a significant figure in modern paganism and Wicca, where she is revered as a powerful goddess of magic and transformation.

Resources

1. "Theogony" by Hesiod: Provides an account of Hekate's origins and her esteemed position among the gods.

37

HEL

(NORSE)

Description

Hel is a prominent figure in Norse mythology, known as the ruler of the underworld, also named Hel. She is often depicted as a fearsome and somber entity, with a striking appearance that is half living, often described as a beautiful woman, and half dead, resembling a decayed corpse. Her domain is a cold, shadowy place where she presides over the souls of those who did not die a heroic or notable death.

Origin

Hel is the daughter of the trickster god Loki and the giantess Angrboda, making her the sister of the wolf Fenrir and the serpent Jormungandr. Due to her lineage and her formidable nature, the gods deemed it necessary to confine her to the underworld to prevent her from causing trouble in the realm of the living.

Lore

Hel plays a crucial role in Norse eschatology and the fate of the dead:

- **Baldur's Death**: One of the most famous myths involving Hel is the story of Baldur's death. When Baldur, the beloved god, is killed, his soul descends to Hel's realm. The gods plead with Hel to release him, and she agrees to do so only if everything in the world weeps for Baldur. When one being, the giantess Thokk (believed to be Loki in disguise), refuses to weep, Hel keeps Baldur in her realm, illustrating her unwavering nature.
- **Ragnarök**: During Ragnarök, the end of the world in Norse mythology, Hel's realm plays a significant role. It is prophesied that she will release the dead to join the forces of chaos in the final battle against the gods.

Additional Facts

- **Symbolism of Duality**: Hel's appearance, half-living and half-dead, symbolizes the duality of life and death, and the thin boundary between the two.
- **Not Evil**: Despite her grim role, Hel is not considered evil in Norse mythology. She is a necessary figure who oversees the natural order of death.
- **Hel's Realm**: Unlike the Christian concept of Hell, Hel's domain is not a place of eternal torment but rather a cold, desolate abode for the dead.

Resources

1. "Prose Edda" by Snorri Sturluson: A primary source for Norse myths, including detailed accounts of Hel.

38

HERA

(GREEK)

Description

Hera is the Greek goddess of marriage, women, childbirth, and family. As the queen of the Olympian gods, she is often depicted as a regal and majestic figure, wearing a crown or diadem and holding a scepter. Hera is frequently portrayed with a peacock, her sacred animal, symbolizing her beauty and royalty. Despite her dignified appearance, she is known for her fierce temper and jealousy, especially regarding her husband Zeus's numerous affairs.

Origin

Hera is one of the twelve Olympian deities and the daughter of the Titans Cronus and Rhea. She is the sister and wife of Zeus, the king of the gods. Hera's marriage to Zeus is central to her role in Greek mythology, emphasizing her dominion over marriage and the sanctity of the marital bond. Her Roman counterpart is Juno, who shares many of her attributes and aspects.

Lore

Hera features prominently in many Greek myths, often highlighting her protective nature over marriage and her vengeful side against those who cross her:

- **Marriage to Zeus**: Hera's marriage to Zeus was marked by both love and conflict. Despite their union being a symbol of divine marriage, Zeus's infidelity led to numerous conflicts between them. Hera's attempts to punish Zeus's lovers and their offspring are well-documented in myth.
- **The Trojan War**: Hera played a significant role in the events leading up to and during the Trojan War. Offended by Paris's judgment in favor of Aphrodite over herself and Athena, Hera supported the Greeks in the war and used her influence to sway events in their favor.

Additional Facts

- **Peacock Symbolism**: The peacock is sacred to Hera. According to myth, the peacock's eyes in its feathers were placed there by Hera, commemorating her loyal watchman Argus.
- **Jealous Nature**: Hera's jealousy is a recurring theme in myths, often driving her actions against Zeus's lovers and illegitimate children. This trait underscores her commitment to marital fidelity, albeit in a vengeful manner.

Resources

1. "The Iliad" by Homer: Provides numerous references to Hera's role in the Trojan War and her relationships.

39

HERCULES

(GREEK)

Description

Heracles, known as Hercules in Roman mythology, is one of the most celebrated heroes in Greek mythology. He is renowned for his extraordinary strength, bravery, and numerous heroic deeds. Often depicted as a muscular, bearded man wielding a club and wearing a lion's skin (the Nemean Lion's hide), Heracles embodies the ideal of heroism and physical prowess.

Origin

Heracles is the son of Zeus, the king of the gods, and Alcmene, a mortal woman. His divine parentage endowed him with superhuman strength and abilities. Hera, Zeus's wife, harbored a deep-seated hatred for Heracles due to her husband's infidelity, which influenced many of the challenges he faced throughout his life.

Lore

Heracles is best known for his Twelve Labors, a series of tasks he was forced to complete as penance for killing his wife and children in a fit of madness induced by Hera.

Heracles' adventures extend beyond the Twelve Labors, involving numerous other feats and battles, including the rescue of Prometheus, participation in the Argonauts' expedition, and various encounters with gods and mortals.

Additional Facts

- **Divine Wrath and Redemption**: Hera's relentless persecution of Heracles underscores the theme of divine retribution and the hero's quest for redemption.
- **Iconic Symbols**: Heracles' club and lion's skin are iconic symbols of his strength and heroic status.
- **Heracles' Death and Apotheosis**: After a life filled with challenges, Heracles was poisoned by his wife Deianira with a garment soaked in the blood of the centaur Nessus. In agony, he built his own funeral pyre and was ultimately granted immortality, ascending to Olympus as a god.
- **Cult and Worship**: Heracles was worshipped as both a hero and a god throughout the ancient Greek world, with numerous temples and festivals dedicated to him.
- **Cultural Legacy**: Heracles' stories have been retold in various forms of art, literature, and modern media, cementing his status as a timeless symbol of strength and resilience.

Resources

1. "The Library" by Apollodorus: A comprehensive source of Greek myths, including the exploits of Heracles.

40

HERMES

(GREEK)

Description

Hermes is the Greek god of commerce, communication, travel, and thievery. Known for his speed and cunning, he is often depicted as a youthful and athletic figure, wearing winged sandals (talaria), a winged hat (petasos), and carrying a caduceus, a staff entwined with two snakes. Hermes serves as the messenger of the gods and a guide for souls traveling to the underworld.

Origin

Hermes is the son of Zeus, the king of the gods, and Maia, one of the Pleiades and daughter of the Titan Atlas. His Roman counterpart is Mercury. From his birth, Hermes demonstrated his cleverness and resourcefulness, traits that would define his role in Greek mythology.

Lore

Hermes is involved in many myths, often highlighting his roles as a messenger, trickster, and guide:

- **Messenger of the Gods**: Hermes is known for his speed and ability to move freely between the mortal and divine worlds. He delivers messages for Zeus and other gods, ensuring communication across realms.
- **Birth and Early Feats**: Shortly after his birth, Hermes showed his mischievous nature by stealing Apollo's cattle. To cover his tracks, he invented the lyre from a tortoise shell and gifted it to Apollo, who in return allowed him to keep the cattle. This story highlights Hermes' inventive and diplomatic skills.
- **Guide of Souls (Psychopomp)**: Hermes guides the souls of the deceased to the underworld, ensuring they reach their final resting place. This role emphasizes his connection to the boundary between life and death.
- **Invention of the Lyre**: One of Hermes' most famous myths involves the creation of the lyre. He made the instrument from a tortoise shell, reeds, ox hide, and sheep-gut strings. This invention showcased his ingenuity and musical talent.

Additional Facts

- **Protector of Travelers**: Hermes is the patron of travelers, ensuring their safe passage. His role as a guide extends to all who journey, whether by land, sea, or air.
- **God of Boundaries**: Hermes oversees boundaries and transitions, both physical and metaphorical. He is associated with doorways, roads, and trade routes.

Resources

1. "The Iliad" and "The Odyssey" by Homer.

41

HORUS

(Egyptian)

Description

Horus is one of the most significant deities in ancient Egyptian mythology, known as the god of the sky, war, and kingship. He is typically depicted as a falcon or as a man with the head of a falcon, often wearing the double crown of Egypt, symbolizing his rule over both Upper and Lower Egypt. Horus is associated with the sun and the moon, his right eye representing the sun and his left eye the moon.

Origin

Horus is the son of Osiris, the god of the afterlife, and Isis, the goddess of magic and motherhood. According to myth, after Osiris was murdered by his brother Seth, Isis resurrected Osiris long enough to conceive Horus. Horus was then raised in secret to protect him from Seth. As he grew, Horus became the avenger of his father's death, ultimately defeating Seth to claim the throne of Egypt.

Lore

Horus plays a central role in many Egyptian myths, particularly in the themes of kingship, vengeance, and the struggle between order and chaos:

- **The Osiris Myth**: In this foundational myth, Horus avenges his father's murder by battling his uncle Seth. The struggle between Horus and Seth symbolizes the eternal conflict between order (ma'at) and chaos (isfet). After a series of trials and battles, Horus emerges victorious and is declared the rightful king of Egypt.

- **The Eye of Horus**: One of the most famous symbols in Egyptian mythology, the Eye of Horus (Wedjat), represents protection, royal power, and good health. According to myth, during his battles with Seth, Horus lost his left eye, which was later restored by Thoth, the god of wisdom. The Eye of Horus became a powerful amulet symbolizing healing and protection.

- **Horus as King**: Horus is often depicted as the divine protector of the pharaoh, embodying the ideal ruler. Pharaohs were considered the earthly incarnation of Horus, ensuring the continuity of ma'at and the prosperity of Egypt.

Additional Facts

- **Dual Nature**: Horus has multiple aspects, including Horus the Elder, a primordial sky god, and Horus the Younger, the son of Osiris and Isis, emphasizing his complex nature and wide-ranging influence.

- **Symbolism**: The falcon, representing Horus, symbolizes keen vision and swift action. His association with the sky links him to the sun and the moon, emphasizing his dominion over day and night.

Resources

1. "The Oxford History of Ancient Egypt" by Ian Shaw: The significance of Horus in Egyptian culture.

42

HYDRA

(Greek)

Description

The Hydra is a fearsome multi-headed serpent-like monster from Greek mythology. It is often depicted as a gigantic creature with numerous snake-like heads, each capable of growing back if severed. The Hydra's breath and blood are said to be highly toxic, making it a lethal adversary. It resides in the swamps or marshes, most famously in the region of Lerna.

Origin

The Hydra is one of the offspring of Typhon and Echidna, two of the most terrifying monsters in Greek mythology. Typhon is a giant serpentine creature, while Echidna is a half-woman, half-snake. The Hydra's siblings include other notorious monsters such as Cerberus, the Chimera, and the Sphinx.

Lore

The most famous myth involving the Hydra is its battle with the hero Heracles (Hercules) during his Twelve Labors:

- **The Second Labor of Heracles**: Heracles was tasked with slaying the Hydra as his second labor. The Hydra lived in the swamps of Lerna, terrorizing the surrounding countryside. Each time Heracles cut off one of the Hydra's heads, two more would grow back in its place. With the help of his nephew Iolaus, Heracles used a torch to cauterize the neck stumps after decapitation, preventing the heads from regenerating. Eventually, Heracles managed to slay the Hydra and dipped his arrows in its poisonous blood, which would later prove useful in other labors.

Additional Facts

- **Toxic Blood and Breath**: The Hydra's blood and breath were highly poisonous. Heracles' use of the Hydra's blood to poison his arrows highlights its lethal nature.
- **Lernaean Hydra**: The swampy area of Lerna, where the Hydra lived, was considered an entrance to the underworld in ancient Greek beliefs, further emphasizing the creature's connection to death and the afterlife.
- **Eternal Adversary**: The Hydra's ability to regenerate its heads has made it a recurring symbol for seemingly insurmountable challenges, often used metaphorically in various contexts.

Resources

1. "Greek Myths" by Robert Graves: A comprehensive collection of Greek myths, including the story of Heracles and the Hydra.

43

IMP

(EUROPEAN)

Description

Imps are small, mischievous creatures found in various mythologies and folklore, often associated with pranks and minor troublemaking. They are typically depicted as tiny, humanoid beings with exaggerated features, such as pointed ears, sharp teeth, and a devilish grin. Imps are known for their playful and sometimes malevolent behavior, which can range from harmless pranks to more serious acts of mischief.

Origin

The concept of imps has roots in European folklore, particularly in medieval and Renaissance periods. The word "imp" is derived from the Old English "impa," meaning "young shoot" or "graft." Originally, the term referred to offspring or progeny, but it later came to denote small, supernatural beings associated with mischief and trickery.

Lore

Imps feature prominently in various cultural mythologies and literary works:

1. **Medieval European Folklore**: In medieval times, imps were often depicted as attendants or familiars to witches and wizards. They were believed to be minor demons or spirits that could be summoned and controlled by practitioners of magic. Imps were thought to assist their masters in casting spells and performing other magical tasks, though they often had a mind of their own and could cause trouble.

2. **Renaissance and Enlightenment**: During the Renaissance and Enlightenment periods, imps were portrayed in literature and art as playful, mischievous creatures. They were often depicted in the margins of manuscripts and paintings, causing minor chaos and engaging in humorous antics.

- **Abilities**: Imps are often endowed with minor magical abilities, such as invisibility, shapeshifting, or the power to cause minor accidents or mishaps.

Additional Facts

- **Symbolism**: Imps are often used symbolically to represent minor evil, mischief, or the unpredictable nature of life. They can also symbolize the trickster archetype, a common figure in mythology and folklore.

- **Familiar Spirits**: In some traditions, imps are considered familiar spirits, serving witches or sorcerers. They are believed to be bound to their master's will, though they often retain their mischievous tendencies.

Resources

1. "The Encyclopedia of Spirits" by Judika Illes: A comprehensive look at imps and sprites.

44

IZANAGI

(JAPANESE)

Description

Izanagi, whose name means "He Who Invites," is a primordial deity in Japanese mythology. He is often depicted as a powerful, divine figure wielding a spear adorned with jewels, known as the Ame-no-Nuhoko (Heavenly Jeweled Spear). Izanagi is revered as the father of many gods and the progenitor of the Japanese archipelago.

Origin

Izanagi and his sister-wife, Izanami, are central figures in the creation myths of Shintoism, the indigenous spirituality of Japan. They are among the last of the kami (deities) to emerge from the chaos that existed before the world was formed. These myths are primarily recorded in two ancient texts: the "Kojiki" (Records of Ancient Matters) and the "Nihon Shoki" (Chronicles of Japan).

Lore

Izanagi's myths revolve around creation, death, and purification:

- **Creation of Japan**: Izanagi and Izanami were commanded by the primordial gods to create the land. Using the Ame-no-Nuhoko, they stirred the chaotic waters, and as they lifted the spear, droplets fell and formed the first island, Onogoro. They descended to this island and performed a ritual to marry and procreate. Their union produced the islands of Japan and many other deities.
- **Death of Izanami**: Tragedy struck when Izanami died giving birth to Kagutsuchi, the fire god. Overcome with grief, Izanagi decided to retrieve her from Yomi, the land of the dead. He found her, but she had already eaten the food of the underworld and could not return. When he saw her decayed form, he fled in horror. Enraged, Izanami sent spirits to chase him, but Izanagi escaped and sealed the entrance to Yomi with a large boulder.

Additional Facts

- **Duality of Creation and Death**: Izanagi's story highlights the dual nature of life and death, creation and decay, emphasizing the cycles of nature.
- **Symbolism of Purification**: The purification ritual performed by Izanagi is foundational in Shinto practices, symbolizing the cleansing of spiritual impurities.

Resources

1. "Kojiki" (Records of Ancient Matters): The oldest chronicle of Japanese myths.

45

IZANAMI

(JAPANESE)

Description

Izanami, whose name means "She Who Invites," is a primordial goddess in Japanese mythology. She is often depicted as a beautiful and majestic figure, embodying the feminine aspects of creation and life. Izanami is revered as the mother of many gods and the co-creator of the Japanese archipelago alongside her brother and husband, Izanagi.

Origin

Izanami and Izanagi are central figures in the Shinto creation myth. They are among the last of the kami (deities) to emerge from the primordial chaos. Their story is primarily recorded in two ancient texts: the "Kojiki" (Records of Ancient Matters) and the "Nihon Shoki" (Chronicles of Japan).

Lore

Izanami's myths revolve around themes of creation, death, and transformation:

- **Creation of Japan**: Izanami and Izanagi were tasked by the primordial gods to create the land. Using the Ame-no-Nuhoko (Heavenly Jeweled Spear), they stirred the chaotic waters, and as they lifted the spear, droplets fell and formed the first island, Onogoro. They descended to this island and performed a ritual to marry and procreate. Their union produced the islands of Japan and many other deities.
- **Death of Izanami**: Tragedy struck when Izanami died giving birth to Kagutsuchi, the fire god. Her death deeply grieved Izanagi, who decided to descend to Yomi, the land of the dead, to retrieve her. In Yomi, Izanagi found Izanami, but she had already consumed the food of the underworld and could not return. Izanagi saw her decayed form and fled in horror, sealing the entrance to Yomi with a large boulder. This act separated the worlds of the living and the dead.
- **Transformation into a Death Deity**: After her death and descent into Yomi, Izanami became a powerful deity of death. She vowed to take a thousand lives every day, to which Izanagi responded that he would ensure the birth of fifteen hundred new lives each day, symbolizing the cycle of life and death.

Additional Facts

- **Symbolism of Life and Death**: Izanami's story highlights the dual nature of creation and destruction, emphasizing the interconnectedness of life and death.

Resources

1. "Kojiki" (Records of Ancient Matters): The oldest chronicle of Japanese myths, detailing Izanami and Izanagi.

46

JORMUNGANDR

(NORSE)

Description

Jormungandr, also known as the Midgard Serpent or the World Serpent, is a colossal sea serpent in Norse mythology. He is often depicted as an enormous, fearsome creature that encircles Midgard (Earth), holding his own tail in his mouth. Jormungandr's immense size and power make him one of the most formidable beings in Norse myth.

Origin

Jormungandr is one of the three children of the trickster god Loki and the giantess Angrboda. His siblings are Fenrir, the monstrous wolf, and Hel, the ruler of the underworld. Due to a prophecy that Loki's children would bring great misfortune, the gods took preventive measures against them. Odin, the chief of the gods, cast Jormungandr into the ocean that surrounds Midgard, where he grew so large that he encircled the world.

Lore

Jormungandr plays a crucial role in several Norse myths, often highlighting themes of fate and the cyclical nature of time:

- **The Binding of Fenrir**: Alongside his siblings, Jormungandr was perceived as a threat to the gods. While Fenrir was bound, Jormungandr was thrown into the ocean to prevent him from causing harm.
- **Ragnarök**: Jormungandr is destined to play a significant role in Ragnarök, the end of the world. According to prophecy, he will emerge from the ocean, poisoning the sky and sea with his venom. He and Thor will face each other in a final battle, during which Thor will kill Jormungandr but will succumb to the serpent's venom shortly after, marking the end of the old world and the beginning of a new cycle.

Additional Facts

- **Immense Size**: Jormungandr's ability to encircle the Earth emphasizes his immense size and the grand scale of Norse cosmology.
- **Foe of Thor**: The recurring theme of conflict between Thor and Jormungandr underscores the eternal struggle between order (represented by Thor) and chaos (embodied by Jormungandr).
- **Runic Representation**: In some interpretations, Jormungandr is associated with the Elder Futhark rune "Jera," symbolizing the cycle of the year and the harvest, reflecting his role in the cyclical events of Norse mythology.

Resources

1. "The Prose Edda" by Snorri Sturluson: A primary source for Norse myths.

47

KALI

(HINDU)

Description

Kali is a prominent goddess in Hindu mythology, known for her fierce and powerful nature. She is often depicted with a dark or black complexion, wearing a garland of skulls, a skirt of severed arms, and a lolling tongue. Kali is typically shown with multiple arms, each holding a weapon or a severed head, symbolizing her role as a destroyer of evil forces. Despite her fearsome appearance, she is also revered as a protective mother figure and a symbol of time and change.

Origin

Kali's origins can be traced back to ancient texts such as the "Devi Mahatmya," where she emerges from the goddess Durga during a battle against demonic forces. She is considered a manifestation of Durga's wrath and power. Kali is also closely associated with Shiva, one of the principal deities of Hinduism. In some stories, she is depicted as Shiva's consort and his female counterpart, embodying his destructive and transformative aspects.

Lore

Kali's myths are rich with symbolism and emphasize her role as a warrior and a protector:

- **Battle with Demons**: One of the most famous myths involving Kali is her battle against the demon Raktabija. According to the "Devi Mahatmya," every drop of Raktabija's blood that touched the ground would spawn a new demon. To prevent this, Kali licked up his blood before it could fall, eventually defeating him and his army.

- **The Dance of Destruction**: In another well-known story, Kali becomes so consumed with bloodlust during a battle that she begins a frenzied dance of destruction. To stop her, Shiva lies down among the corpses on the battlefield. When Kali steps on him, she realizes her mistake and calms down, which symbolizes the balance between creation and destruction.

- **Kali and Shiva**: Kali is often depicted standing or dancing on Shiva's prone body, representing the dynamic and interdependent relationship between destruction (Kali) and regeneration (Shiva).

Additional Facts

- **Symbolism of Kali**: Kali's dark complexion symbolizes the eternal darkness from which all things emerge and into which all things will ultimately return. Her garland of skulls represents the cycle of life, death, and rebirth, while her weapons signify the destruction of evil and ignorance.

- **Role as a Mother Goddess**: Despite her terrifying form, Kali is also worshipped as a compassionate mother who protects her devotees from harm and grants them liberation (moksha). She embodies both maternal love and fierce protection.

Resources

1. "Devi Maatmya" (The Glory of the Goddess): An important text from the Markandeya Purana.

48

THE KRAKEN

(SCANDINAVIAN)

Description

The Kraken is a legendary sea monster of enormous size, often depicted as a giant squid or octopus. According to myth, it dwells off the coasts of Norway and Greenland and terrorizes sailors by emerging from the depths to drag entire ships and their crews into the ocean. Its massive tentacles, capable of wrapping around vessels and pulling them under, make the Kraken one of the most fearsome creatures in maritime folklore.

Origin

The Kraken originates from Scandinavian folklore, particularly Norwegian and Icelandic sagas. It is often described in old seafarers' tales and natural histories, which blended myth with observations of real marine life, such as large squid and octopuses. The word "Kraken" comes from the Norwegian word "krake," meaning an unhealthy animal or something twisted.

Lore

The Kraken is associated with various maritime legends and stories:

- **The Monstrous Cephalopod**: According to legend, the Kraken can grow to a size so large that its body can be mistaken for an island. Sailors would often describe seeing the creature rise from the sea, creating massive whirlpools capable of capsizing ships.
- **Bishop Erik Pontoppidan**: In the 18th century, Bishop Erik Pontoppidan of Norway wrote about the Kraken in his book "The Natural History of Norway." He described it as a creature so large that when it surfaced, it appeared to be a series of small islands. He also suggested that its spouting water could resemble geysers.
- **Encounters with Sailors**: Many old sailor tales describe encounters with the Kraken. These stories often involve the creature wrapping its tentacles around ships, pulling them into the ocean depths, and creating whirlpools to drown sailors.

Additional Facts

- **Symbol of the Unknown**: The Kraken represents the fear of the unknown and the dangers lurking beneath the ocean's surface, symbolizing the unpredictability and power of the sea.
- **Nautical Charts**: In historical nautical charts, the Kraken and other sea monsters were often depicted in areas that were uncharted or considered dangerous, serving as a warning to sailors.

Resources

1. "The Natural History of Norway" by Erik Pontoppidan: A key historical source that describes the Kraken.

49

KRAMPUS

(EUROPEAN)

Description

Krampus is a figure from Central European folklore, often depicted as a horned, anthropomorphic creature with a menacing appearance. He is typically portrayed with dark, shaggy fur, cloven hooves, and goat-like horns. Krampus is known for his long, pointed tongue and sharp teeth, carrying chains and bells, and a bundle of birch sticks used to swat naughty children. In some depictions, he also carries a sack or basket on his back to take away misbehaving children.

Origin

The origins of Krampus date back to pre-Christian Alpine traditions. His name is derived from the German word "krampen," meaning "claw." Krampus is believed to be a pagan figure that predates the spread of Christianity in Europe, possibly linked to ancient pagan rituals celebrating the winter solstice. Over time, Krampus was incorporated into Christian traditions, particularly in regions such as Austria, Bavaria, Croatia, Slovenia, and Northern Italy.

Lore

Krampus is most commonly associated with the celebration of Krampusnacht, or Krampus Night, which occurs on the evening of December 5th, the night before the Feast of St. Nicholas. While St. Nicholas rewards well-behaved children with gifts and treats, Krampus punishes those who have been naughty. The lore surrounding Krampus includes several key elements:

1. **Companion of St. Nicholas**: Krampus accompanies St. Nicholas during his rounds to visit children. While St. Nicholas offers gifts and goodwill, Krampus deals with those who have misbehaved, using his birch sticks to swat them or stuffing them into his sack to take them away.

2. **Krampuslauf (Krampus Run)**: In many towns and cities, people participate in Krampuslauf, where individuals dressed as Krampus parade through the streets, often chasing spectators and engaging in playful, yet frightening antics.

3. **Regional Variations**: Krampus traditions vary by region. In some areas, he is part of a larger entourage of dark companions to St. Nicholas, including figures like Knecht Ruprecht and Perchten.

Additional Facts

- **Symbolism**: Krampus serves as a symbol of the duality of the holiday season, representing both the joyous and the darker, more punitive aspects of the time.

Resources

1. Smithsonian Magazine: Offers insights into the origins and modern revival of "Krampus".

50

KRISHNA

(HINDU)

Description

Krishna is one of the most revered deities in Hinduism, known for his roles as a divine hero, supreme god, and the beloved god of compassion, tenderness, and love. He is often depicted as a young, blue-skinned boy playing a flute, or as a handsome prince engaged in heroic exploits. Krishna's life and teachings have profoundly influenced Indian culture, art, and religion.

Origin

Krishna is considered the eighth avatar of Vishnu, the preserver god in the Hindu trinity. He was born to Devaki and Vasudeva in the Yadava clan, under miraculous circumstances, to destroy the tyrant king Kamsa, who was prophesied to be killed by Devaki's eighth son. Krishna's birth and childhood are filled with miraculous events and divine interventions, symbolizing the triumph of good over evil.

Lore

Krishna's life is chronicled in various Hindu texts, including the "Bhagavata Purana," the "Mahabharata," and the "Harivamsa." Key aspects of his lore include:

- **Bhagavad Gita**: One of the most significant episodes in Krishna's life is his role in the Mahabharata, particularly during the Kurukshetra War. In the "Bhagavad Gita," Krishna serves as the charioteer and guide to the warrior prince Arjuna, delivering profound spiritual teachings on duty, righteousness, and devotion. This scripture is considered one of the most important philosophical texts in Hinduism.
- **Defeating Kamsa and Other Demons**: Krishna's life is also marked by numerous heroic deeds, including the defeat of his evil uncle Kamsa and other demons who threatened the world. These stories emphasize his role as a protector and preserver of dharma (righteousness).

Additional Facts

- **Symbol of Divine Love:** Krishna's playful and loving interactions, especially with Radha and the gopis, symbolize the joy and beauty of divine love and devotion.
- **Versatile Depictions**: Krishna is depicted in various forms, from the mischievous child "Makhan Chor" (butter thief) to the wise and compassionate teacher in the "Bhagavad Gita."

Resources

1. "Krishna: The Man and His Philosophy" by Osho: Offers a modern interpretation of Krishna's life and teachings.

51

LEPRECHAUN

(Celtic)

Description

Leprechauns are small, fairy-like creatures from Irish folklore, often depicted as mischievous old men dressed in green coats and hats. They are typically solitary beings known for their trickery and cunning. Leprechauns are also associated with wealth, as they are said to possess hidden pots of gold.

Origin

The origin of leprechauns can be traced back to Celtic mythology. The word "leprechaun" is derived from the Old Irish term "luchorpán," meaning "small body." Originally, they were considered part of the Tuatha Dé Danann, a supernatural race in Irish mythology. Over time, leprechauns evolved into the solitary, trickster figures recognized in folklore today.

Leprechauns are believed to be shoemakers or cobblers by trade, often found mending shoes. This association with shoemaking is one of the defining characteristics of leprechauns in folklore.

Lore

Leprechaun lore is rich with tales of their mischievous behavior and hidden treasures:

- **Trickery**: Leprechauns are notorious for playing tricks on humans. They enjoy causing mischief and are often depicted as cunning and sly.
- **Wealth**: Leprechauns are said to hide pots of gold at the end of rainbows. If captured by a human, a leprechaun might grant three wishes in exchange for their release. However, they often use their wit to escape without giving away their gold.
- **Appearance**: Traditional depictions of leprechauns show them as small, bearded men dressed in green coats, hats, and buckled shoes. They often carry a shillelagh, a type of wooden walking stick.

Additional Facts

1. **Symbolism**: In modern times, leprechauns have become symbols of Irish culture and St. Patrick's Day celebrations. Their image is widely used in Irish-themed merchandise and advertising.
2. **Regional Variations**: In some regional tales, leprechauns are confused with other fairy beings such as clurichauns, who are similar in appearance but are known for causing more trouble and mischief, particularly related to alcohol.

Resources

1. "Leprechauns and Irish Folklore" by Mary Pope Osborne.

52

LOKI

(NORSE)

Description

Loki is a complex and multifaceted deity in Norse mythology, known for his cunning, mischief, and shape-shifting abilities. He is often depicted as a handsome yet mischievous figure, embodying both the qualities of a trickster and a troublemaker. Loki's actions frequently bring chaos and conflict, but he also possesses a clever and resourceful nature that sometimes benefits the gods.

Origin

Loki's origins are somewhat ambiguous in Norse mythology. He is the son of the giants Farbauti and Laufey, making him of Jotun (giant) descent. Despite his giant heritage, Loki is counted among the Aesir, the principal gods of the Norse pantheon, due to his close relationship with Odin and Thor. His role within the pantheon is often contradictory, as he oscillates between aiding and undermining the gods.

Lore

Loki is involved in numerous myths, often serving as a catalyst for both trouble and resolution:

- **The Binding of Fenrir**: Loki is the father of several monstrous offspring, including Fenrir, the giant wolf. To prevent Fenrir from wreaking havoc, the gods decide to bind him. Despite Loki's initial protests, Fenrir is ultimately restrained, setting the stage for future conflict.

- **Punishment and Binding**: After causing Balder's death, Loki is punished by being bound in a cave with a serpent positioned above him, dripping venom onto his face. His wife, Sigyn, stays by his side, catching the venom in a bowl. However, when she empties the bowl, the venom drips onto Loki, causing him to writhe in pain, which is said to cause earthquakes.

- **Ragnarök**: During Ragnarök, the prophesied end of the world, Loki will break free from his bonds and lead the giants and other enemies of the gods in a final battle against the Aesir. He will confront Heimdall, the guardian of the Bifrost bridge, and the two will ultimately kill each other.

Additional Facts

- **Ambivalent Nature**: Loki embodies the duality of creation and destruction, loyalty and betrayal, reflecting the complex and often contradictory aspects of human nature.

- **Relationships with the Gods**: Despite his many transgressions, Loki's relationships with other gods, particularly Thor, are marked by camaraderie and mutual respect, adding depth to his character.

Resources

1. "The Prose Edda" by Snorri Sturluson: A primary source for Norse myths, including detailed accounts of Loki.

53

MAGE (WZARD, SORCERER)

(EUROPEAN, EGYPTIAN, GREEK, ROMAN)

Description

Mages, also known as wizards, sorcerers, or magicians, are mythical figures renowned for their mastery of magical arts and supernatural powers. Often depicted as wise, elderly figures with long beards and robes adorned with arcane symbols, mages possess knowledge of spells, enchantments, and ancient wisdom. They are frequently associated with elements of alchemy, astrology, and divination, and play pivotal roles in mythological narratives as advisors, protectors, and powerful adversaries.

Origin

The concept of mages has ancient roots, with origins in various cultures and mythologies around the world. In ancient Egypt, priests and magicians wielded considerable influence through their knowledge of spells and rituals. In Mesopotamian mythology, wise men known as "apkallu" were considered demigods and sages who brought knowledge to humanity. The archetype of the mage evolved through Greco-Roman traditions, medieval European folklore, and other cultural influences, solidifying their place in mythological and literary traditions.

Lore

Mages feature prominently in numerous myths and legends, often embodying themes of wisdom, power, and the pursuit of knowledge:

- **Merlin**: Perhaps the most famous mage in Western mythology, Merlin is a central figure in Arthurian legend. As the advisor to King Arthur, Merlin's knowledge of magic and prophecy plays a crucial role in the king's rise and reign. Merlin is often depicted as a mentor figure, guiding Arthur with his profound wisdom and magical prowess.

Additional Facts

- **Alchemy and the Philosopher's Stone**: Many mages are associated with the pursuit of alchemy, the ancient practice of transforming base metals into gold and seeking the elixir of life. The legendary Philosopher's Stone is a central symbol in alchemical lore, representing ultimate knowledge and immortality.
- **Symbols and Tools**: Mages are often depicted with various magical tools and symbols, such as staffs, wands, crystal balls, and grimoires (books of magic). These items signify their connection to mystical forces and their ability to channel magical energy.
- **Dual Nature**: The dual nature of magic is a common theme in mage lore, illustrating how magical power can be used for both good and evil. This duality highlights the ethical dilemmas and responsibilities that come with wielding such power.

Resources

1. "The Once and Future King" by T.H. White: A modern retelling of Arthurian legends, featuring Merlin.

54

MANTICORE

(PERSIAN)

Description

The manticore is a mythical creature with origins in Persian legend, known for its fearsome appearance and deadly nature. It is often depicted as having the body of a lion, the head of a human (sometimes with sharp, predatory teeth), and a tail that can be either that of a dragon or a scorpion, capable of shooting venomous spines. The manticore embodies the combination of multiple predatory traits, making it a symbol of terror and danger.

Origin

The term "manticore" comes from the Persian word "mardyakhor," meaning "man-eater." The creature was first described in ancient Persian mythology and later adopted into Greek and Roman mythologies through the works of writers such as Ctesias, Pliny the Elder, and later medieval bestiaries. The manticore's legend spread across cultures, each adding unique attributes to its description.

Lore

The manticore is a creature of both legend and terror, often associated with themes of danger and the unknown:

- **Persian Mythology**: In its original Persian context, the manticore was a deadly predator with a voracious appetite for human flesh. It was believed to inhabit the jungles of India, lurking and preying on those who wandered into its territory.
- **Greek and Roman Accounts**: Greek and Roman authors, including Ctesias and Pliny the Elder, described the manticore as a monstrous hybrid with the body of a red lion, a human head with three rows of sharp teeth, and a tail capable of shooting venomous spines. These accounts often emphasized the creature's lethality and its man-eating nature.
- **Medieval Bestiaries**: During the medieval period, the manticore was featured in bestiaries—compendiums of real and mythical animals used to teach moral lessons.

Additional Facts

- **Symbolism of Fear and Danger**: The manticore's frightening appearance and deadly abilities symbolize the unknown dangers that lurk beyond the familiar world. It represents the ultimate predator, combining the most fearsome attributes of multiple animals.
- **Venomous Spines**: One of the manticore's most distinctive features is its tail, which can shoot venomous spines or quills, similar to those of a porcupine or scorpion. This ability adds to its terrifying reputation as an inescapable threat.

Resources

1. "Natural History" by Pliny the Elder: One of the earliest detailed accounts of the manticore.

55

MEDUSA

(GREEK)

Description

Medusa is one of the most iconic figures in Greek mythology, known for her hair of living snakes and her ability to turn anyone who gazes directly at her into stone. She is often depicted as a winged woman with a fearsome visage, snake hair, and sometimes with a serpentine lower body. Despite her terrifying appearance, Medusa's story is one of tragedy and transformation.

Origin

Medusa is one of the three Gorgons, the daughters of the sea deities Phorcys and Ceto. Unlike her immortal sisters, Stheno and Euryale, Medusa was mortal. According to various myths, Medusa was originally a beautiful maiden who was transformed into a monster as a result of divine punishment.

Lore

Medusa's story is rich with themes of beauty, punishment, and heroism:

- **Transformation**: In Ovid's "Metamorphoses," Medusa was a beautiful maiden and a priestess in Athena's temple. Poseidon, the god of the sea, was captivated by her beauty and desecrated Athena's temple by attacking Medusa there. Enraged, Athena transformed Medusa's beautiful hair into serpents and cursed her with a gaze that would turn onlookers to stone.
- **The Hero Perseus**: Medusa's most famous myth involves the hero Perseus, who was tasked with retrieving her head by King Polydectes. With the help of the gods, Perseus received several magical items: a reflective shield from Athena, winged sandals from Hermes, a sword from Hephaestus, and Hades' helm of invisibility. Using the shield to view Medusa's reflection and avoid direct eye contact, Perseus beheaded her while she slept. From her blood sprang Pegasus, the winged horse, and Chrysaor, a giant wielding a golden sword.
- **Medusa's Head**: After her death, Medusa's head retained its petrifying power. Perseus used it as a weapon in several adventures before giving it to Athena, who placed it on her shield, the Aegis, as a protective emblem.

Additional Facts

- **Symbol of Protection**: Medusa's head, or Gorgoneion, was often used as a protective symbol on shields, armor, and buildings to ward off evil and protect against enemies.

Resources

1. "Metamorphoses" by Ovid: Provides a detailed account of Medusa's transformation and her role in Perseus's myth.
2. "Theogony" by Hesiod: Offers insights into the genealogy of Medusa and her sisters.

56

MERMAID

(ASSYRIAN, GREEK, ROMAN)

Description

Mermaids are mythical sea creatures with the upper body of a human female and the lower body of a fish. They are often depicted as beautiful, enchanting beings with long flowing hair, shimmering scales, and an alluring presence. Mermaids have been a part of maritime folklore for centuries, symbolizing both the beauty and danger of the sea.

Origin

The concept of mermaids can be traced back to ancient civilizations, including the Assyrians, Greeks, and Romans. One of the earliest recorded mermaid legends comes from Assyria around 1000 BCE, where the goddess Atargatis transformed into a mermaid out of shame. In Greek mythology, mermaids are often associated with sirens, who were initially bird-women but later became more like mermaids in folklore.

Lore

Mermaid myths are rich and varied, spanning different cultures and time periods:

- **Sirens of Greek Mythology**: In Homer's "Odyssey," sirens are sea nymphs who lured sailors to their deaths with their enchanting songs. While not originally mermaids, their depiction evolved over time to include mermaid-like characteristics.
- **European Folklore**: In European tales, mermaids are often portrayed as both benevolent and malevolent. They could grant wishes, foretell the future, and bring good luck, but they could also cause shipwrecks and drown sailors. The dual nature of mermaids reflects the unpredictable and mysterious nature of the sea.
- **Selkies and Other Variants**: In Scottish and Irish folklore, selkies are mythical beings that can transform from seals into humans. Similar to mermaids, selkies are associated with the sea and have stories that blend romance and tragedy.

Additional Facts

- **Symbolism of Mermaids**: Mermaids often symbolize the unknown, the subconscious, and the dual nature of human desires. Their enchanting beauty and dangerous allure reflect the sea's ability to give life and take it away.
- **Mermaids in Maritime Folklore**: Sailors' tales of mermaid sightings were common during long voyages. These sightings were sometimes attributed to manatees or dugongs, whose features, seen from a distance, might resemble a mermaid's.

Resources

1. "The Little Mermaid" by Hans Christian Andersen: A classic fairy tale that has inspired countless adaptations and remains a central piece of mermaid lore.

57

MINOTAUR

(GREEK)

Description

The Minotaur is a mythical creature from Greek mythology, known for its unique and fearsome appearance: the body of a man and the head of a bull. This monstrous being was housed in an elaborate labyrinth designed by the skilled craftsman Daedalus and was infamous for its role in the legend of Theseus.

Origin

The Minotaur's origin story is a tale of divine retribution and human folly. It begins with Minos, the king of Crete, who sought to prove his divine right to rule. He prayed to Poseidon to send him a magnificent bull as a sign. Poseidon obliged, with the expectation that Minos would sacrifice the bull in his honor. However, Minos kept the bull for himself, angering Poseidon. In revenge, the sea god cursed Minos's wife, Pasiphae, causing her to fall in love with the bull. From their union, the Minotaur was born.

Lore

The Minotaur's story is intertwined with themes of punishment, heroism, and the struggle between man and beast:

- **The Labyrinth**: Ashamed of the creature and seeking to contain its destructive power, Minos ordered Daedalus to construct a vast labyrinth beneath the palace at Knossos. The labyrinth was so complex that no one could escape it once they entered.
- **Theseus and the Minotaur**: The hero Theseus volunteered to be part of the tribute with the intention of killing the Minotaur and ending the cycle of sacrifice. Before entering the labyrinth, Theseus received a ball of thread from Ariadne, Minos's daughter, to help him find his way out. Theseus used the thread to navigate the labyrinth, slew the Minotaur in combat, and then retraced his path to escape.

Additional Facts

- **Symbolism of the Labyrinth**: The labyrinth represents the complex and often tortuous journey one must undertake to confront and overcome inner demons or challenges.
- **Heroic Feat**: Theseus's slaying of the Minotaur is one of his most celebrated feats, symbolizing the triumph of human courage and intelligence over brute force and monstrosity.
- **Daedalus's Craftsmanship**: The labyrinth itself is a testament to Daedalus's ingenuity and skill as a craftsman and inventor, making it a significant element of the myth.

Resources

1. "Classical Mythology" by Mark P. O. Morford and Robert J. Lenardon: The legend of the Minotaur.

58

THE MUSES

(Greek)

Description

The Muses are nine goddesses from Greek mythology who preside over the arts and sciences. They are often depicted as beautiful, graceful women, each associated with a specific aspect of the creative and intellectual realms. The Muses are considered sources of inspiration for artists, poets, and scholars, and their influence is often invoked at the beginning of literary works and performances.

Origin

The Muses are the daughters of Zeus, the king of the gods, and Mnemosyne, the Titaness of memory. They were born after Zeus and Mnemosyne spent nine consecutive nights together. The Muses reside on Mount Helicon or Mount Parnassus, and they are often associated with the sacred spring of Hippocrene, which was created by the hoof of Pegasus.

Lore

Each Muse is responsible for a different domain of the arts and sciences. The most famous and distinguished being Calliope; she is the Muse of epic poetry, often depicted holding a writing tablet.

The Muses play a crucial role in Greek culture, serving as the embodiment of knowledge and creativity. They were frequently invoked by poets and artists seeking inspiration and guidance in their work.

Additional Facts

- **Hesiod's Invocation**: In his work "Theogony," the poet Hesiod famously invokes the Muses to help him recount the origins of the gods, illustrating their importance in Greek literary tradition.
- **Cults and Worship**: The Muses were worshipped in various regions of Greece, with significant cult centers in Boeotia, particularly on Mount Helicon, and in Pieria, near Mount Olympus.
- **Cultural Influence**: The Muses have had a lasting impact on Western culture, symbolizing artistic inspiration and the pursuit of knowledge. They continue to be referenced in literature, music, and other creative fields.

Resources

1. "Theogony" by Hesiod: This ancient text provides an account of the origins of the gods and includes references to the Muses.
2. "Metamorphoses" by Ovid: A narrative poem that includes various myths involving the Muses.
3. "Greek Religion" by Walter Burkert: This book offers a comprehensive look at Greek religious practices, including the worship of the Muses.

59

ODIN

(NORSE)

Description

Odin is one of the most complex and revered deities in Norse mythology, known as the All-Father and the chief of the Aesir gods. He is associated with wisdom, war, poetry, and the dead. Odin is often depicted as an elderly, one-eyed man with a long beard, wearing a cloak and a wide-brimmed hat. He wields the spear Gungnir and rides the eight-legged horse Sleipnir. His missing eye, sacrificed for wisdom, is one of his most distinguishing features.

Origin

Odin's origins trace back to the early Germanic tribes, where he was worshipped under various names. In Norse mythology, he is the son of Bor and Bestla, making him part of the first generation of Aesir gods. Odin's role as the All-Father signifies his position as the creator and ruler of the cosmos.

Lore

Odin's myths are rich with themes of sacrifice, wisdom, and the pursuit of knowledge:

- **The Creation of the World**: Odin, along with his brothers Vili and Ve, created the world from the body of the giant Ymir. They fashioned the earth from his flesh, the oceans from his blood, the sky from his skull, and the trees from his hair.
- **Ragnarök**: Odin plays a crucial role in the prophecy of Ragnarök, the end of the world. He will lead the Aesir gods in the final battle against the forces of chaos. According to prophecy, Odin will be devoured by the giant wolf Fenrir during this cataclysmic event.

Additional Facts

- Huginn and Muninn: Odin is accompanied by two ravens, Huginn (thought) and Muninn (memory), who fly around the world and bring him information.
- Valhalla: Odin presides over Valhalla, the hall of the slain, where he receives the souls of warriors who died bravely in battle. These warriors, known as the Einherjar, prepare for Ragnarök under his command.
- Shape-Shifting and Magic: Odin is a master of Seidr, a form of Norse magic involving prophecy and shape-shifting. He can transform into various animals and even influence the minds of others.

Resources

1. "Norse Mythology" by Neil Gaiman: A modern retelling of Norse myths, including stories about Odin and his quest for wisdom.

60

ORION

(Greek)

Description

Orion is a legendary figure in Greek mythology, known as a giant and a superb hunter. He is often depicted as a mighty hunter with a club and a lion's pelt, and he is associated with the constellation that bears his name. Orion's tales are filled with adventure, love, and tragedy, reflecting the qualities and pitfalls of heroism.

Origin

Orion's origins vary in different myths, but he is commonly said to be the son of Poseidon, the god of the sea, and Euryale, a daughter of King Minos of Crete. His divine parentage granted him extraordinary abilities, including the power to walk on water. Some versions of the myth suggest that he was born from the earth or a bull hide that had been prayed over and buried by three gods, leading to his epithet "Earth-born."

Lore

Orion's life and adventures are rich with themes of love, pride, and retribution:

- **The Great Hunter**: Orion was renowned for his hunting prowess. He boasted that he could kill any beast on earth, a claim that ultimately led to his downfall. In various myths, he hunted alongside the goddess Artemis and her companion, Leto.
- **Death and Constellation**: Orion's death is recounted in several ways. In one version, Artemis accidentally killed him with an arrow, either due to a challenge or through the machinations of Apollo, who was jealous of their relationship. Another version states that a giant scorpion, sent by Gaia or Artemis herself, killed him. After his death, Orion was placed among the stars by Zeus, forming the constellation Orion. The scorpion was also placed in the sky, becoming the constellation Scorpius, and is said to chase Orion across the heavens.

Additional Facts

- **Orion and the Pleiades**: Orion is often associated with the Pleiades, a group of seven sisters whom he pursued. They were transformed into stars to escape his advances, forming the Pleiades star cluster.
- **Symbol of Heroism and Hubris**: Orion embodies the qualities of a hero and the pitfalls of hubris. His stories reflect the dangers of pride and the tragic outcomes of love and competition among the gods.

Resources

1. "The Odyssey" by Homer: Contains references to Orion's hunting skills and his transformation into a constellation.
2. "Metamorphoses" by Ovid: Offers various accounts of Orion's life, loves, and tragic end.

61

OSIRIS

(EGYPTIAN)

Description

Osiris is one of the most important deities in ancient Egyptian mythology, revered as the god of the afterlife, resurrection, and fertility. He is often depicted as a green-skinned man with a pharaoh's beard, partially wrapped as a mummy, wearing the atef crown (a white crown with two ostrich feathers) and holding a crook and flail, symbols of kingship and dominion.

Origin

Osiris is the son of the earth god Geb and the sky goddess Nut. He is the brother and husband of Isis, and the father of Horus. His siblings also include Set, the god of chaos, and Nephthys. Osiris's story is central to Egyptian religion and is primarily recorded in texts such as the "Pyramid Texts," the "Coffin Texts," and the "Book of the Dead."

Lore

Osiris's myths encompass themes of death, resurrection, and the eternal cycle of life:

- **Rule and Betrayal**: Osiris was a wise and just king who brought civilization, agriculture, and laws to Egypt. His reign was marked by prosperity and order. However, his brother Set, driven by jealousy and a desire for power, plotted against him. Set tricked Osiris into lying in a coffin, which he then sealed and threw into the Nile River.

- **Resurrection by Isis**: Isis, Osiris's devoted wife, searched for and found his body. Using her magical abilities, she resurrected him long enough to conceive their son, Horus. However, Set discovered Osiris's body and dismembered it into fourteen pieces, scattering them across Egypt. Undeterred, Isis recovered all the pieces, except for one (his phallus, which was eaten by a fish), and reassembled his body. Through her efforts, Osiris was brought back to life and became the god of the afterlife.

- **God of the Afterlife**: As the ruler of the underworld, Osiris presides over the judgment of souls. In the Hall of Ma'at, the hearts of the deceased are weighed against the feather of Ma'at (truth and justice). If a soul is found worthy, it is granted eternal life in the Field of Reeds, a paradise resembling the idealized version of Egypt.

Additional Facts

- **Symbol of Fertility**: Osiris is associated with the Nile's annual flooding, which brought fertility and renewal to the land. His green skin represents rebirth and vegetation.

Resources

1. "The Oxford History of Ancient Egypt" by Ian Shaw: Offers a comprehensive overview of ancient Egyptian history and religion, including the significance of Osiris.

62

PEGASUS

(Greek)

Description

Pegasus is one of the most iconic creatures in Greek mythology, known as a magnificent winged horse. Often depicted as pure white and capable of flying, Pegasus embodies both beauty and strength. He is a symbol of poetic inspiration, heroism, and the mystical connection between the earth and the heavens.

Origin

Pegasus's origins are rooted in one of the most famous myths of Greek mythology. He was born from the blood of the Gorgon Medusa after she was beheaded by the hero Perseus. When Perseus severed Medusa's head, Pegasus and his brother Chrysaor sprang forth from her blood. Some myths suggest that Poseidon, the god of the sea, was Pegasus's father, as he had once transformed into a horse to pursue Medusa.

Lore

Pegasus's stories are intertwined with those of gods, heroes, and great feats:

- **Bellerophon and the Chimera**: The most famous myth involving Pegasus is his role in the adventures of the hero Bellerophon. Bellerophon was tasked with slaying the Chimera, a monstrous creature with the body of a lion, the head of a goat, and the tail of a serpent. With the help of Athena, who provided him with a golden bridle, Bellerophon tamed Pegasus and rode him into battle. Together, they soared above the Chimera, and Bellerophon was able to defeat the beast from the air.
- **Mount Helicon and the Muses**: Pegasus is also associated with the Muses and the arts. It is said that Pegasus struck the ground on Mount Helicon with his hoof, creating the Hippocrene spring, which became a source of inspiration for poets and artists. This connection further cemented Pegasus's role as a symbol of creativity and poetic inspiration.

Additional Facts

- **Symbol of Inspiration**: Pegasus is often seen as a symbol of inspiration and artistic creation. His association with the Muses and the Hippocrene spring underscores his role in inspiring poets, writers, and artists.
- **Heroic Companionship**: Pegasus's bond with Bellerophon highlights themes of friendship and loyalty between a hero and his steed, a motif that has been repeated in countless stories and legends.

Resources

1. "The Iliad" by Homer: Contains references to Pegasus, especially in relation to his origins and connections with the gods.
2. "The Greek Myths" by Robert Graves: A thorough retelling of Greek myths, including the stories of Pegasus.

63

PERSEUS

(GREEK)

Description

Perseus is one of the most celebrated heroes in Greek mythology, renowned for his intelligence, bravery, and divine heritage. He is often depicted as a young, handsome man equipped with a reflective shield, a curved sword or sickle (harpe), winged sandals, and sometimes a helm of invisibility. Perseus' most famous myth involves the slaying of the Gorgon Medusa and saving Andromeda from a sea monster.

Origin

Perseus is the son of Zeus, the king of the gods, and Danaë, a mortal princess. According to myth, King Acrisius of Argos, Danaë's father, received a prophecy that he would be killed by his grandson. To prevent this, Acrisius locked Danaë in a bronze chamber. However, Zeus transformed into a golden shower and impregnated her, resulting in the birth of Perseus. When Acrisius discovered Perseus, he cast Danaë and her son into the sea in a chest, but they were rescued by Dictys, a fisherman on the island of Seriphos.

Lore

Perseus' mythology is filled with adventure and heroic deeds:

1. **Slaying Medusa**: King Polydectes of Seriphos, who desired Danaë, tricked Perseus into promising to fetch the head of Medusa, one of the three Gorgons whose gaze could turn people to stone. With the help of Hermes and Athena, Perseus received divine gifts: winged sandals, a reflective shield, a helm of invisibility, and a magical sword. Using the shield to view Medusa's reflection, he safely decapitated her and placed her head in a kibisis (a magical bag).

2. **Rescue of Andromeda**: On his way back, Perseus encountered Andromeda, who was chained to a rock as a sacrifice to a sea monster. Using Medusa's head, he turned the monster to stone and freed Andromeda. He married her and they had several children, including Perses, who is considered the ancestor of the Persian people.

3. **Return to Seriphos**: Upon returning to Seriphos, Perseus used Medusa's head to turn Polydectes and his followers to stone, freeing his mother from the king's advances. He then appointed Dictys as king.

Additional Facts

- **Constellation**: In honor of his heroic deeds, Perseus was placed among the stars as a constellation, which bears his name.

- **Divine Assistance**: Perseus' success is often attributed to the divine assistance he received from gods like Athena and Hermes, emphasizing the theme of divine intervention in human affairs.

Resources

1. Encyclopedia Mythica: Offers detailed information on Perseus' myth and lineage.

64

PHOENIX

(EGYPTIAN, GREEK, ROMAN, CHINESE)

Description

The phoenix is a mythical bird renowned for its stunning beauty and incredible regenerative powers. It is often depicted with vibrant plumage in fiery hues of red, gold, and orange, symbolizing its association with the sun and fire. The phoenix is known for its large size, majestic wingspan, and a regal crest on its head. Its eyes are said to shine with the wisdom of the ages, reflecting its long-lived nature.

Origin

The legend of the phoenix has origins in various ancient cultures, including Egyptian, Greek, Roman, and Chinese mythology. The earliest known references to the phoenix come from ancient Egypt, where it was associated with the sun god Ra and called the Bennu bird. In Greek mythology, the phoenix is closely tied to the concept of cyclical regeneration and immortality. Herodotus, the ancient Greek historian, wrote about the phoenix, describing it as a sacred bird that lived in Arabia and periodically renewed itself.

Lore

The most well-known aspect of the phoenix's mythology is its life cycle. According to legend, the phoenix lives for several hundred years before it senses the approach of death. When the time comes, it builds a nest of aromatic wood and sets it ablaze. The bird is consumed by the flames, but from its ashes, a new phoenix arises, reborn and rejuvenated. This process symbolizes renewal, resurrection, and the eternal cycle of life and death.

In some versions of the myth, the young phoenix gathers the ashes of its predecessor and deposits them in the Egyptian city of Heliopolis, further solidifying its connection to the sun and the theme of rebirth. The phoenix's cycle of death and rebirth has made it a powerful symbol of immortality, resilience, and the enduring nature of life.

Additional Facts

- **Symbolism:** The phoenix is often used as a symbol of renewal, transformation, and the indomitable spirit. It represents the idea that from destruction and decay, new life and vitality can emerge.
- **Cultural Significance:** The phoenix appears in various cultural traditions, each with its unique interpretation. In Chinese mythology, the Fenghuang is a similar bird representing the union of yin and yang and the harmony of the universe.
- **Literary References:** The phoenix has been a popular motif in literature, from ancient texts to modern works. It appears in Ovid's "Metamorphoses," Dante's "Inferno," and J.K. Rowling's "Harry Potter" series, where it is embodied by the loyal bird Fawkes.
- **Modern Interpretations:** In contemporary culture, the phoenix continues to inspire stories, art, and popular media. It is often depicted as a symbol of hope and resilience, especially in times of adversity.

Resources

1. "Mythology: Timeless Tales of Gods and Heroes" by Edith Hamilton: A comprehensive guide to Greek, Roman, and Norse mythology, including the story of the phoenix.
2. "The Phoenix: An Unnatural Biography of a Mythical Beast" by Joseph Nigg: An in-depth exploration of the phoenix myth and its evolution over time.
3. "The Encyclopedia of Mythology: Classical, Celtic, Norse" by Arthur.

65

POSEIDON

(GREEK)

Description

Poseidon is one of the twelve Olympian deities in ancient Greek religion and mythology, primarily known as the god of the sea, earthquakes, storms, and horses. He is often depicted as a mature man with a sturdy build and dark beard, holding a trident, a three-pronged fishing spear. Poseidon is revered as a powerful and temperamental god, capable of both great benevolence and immense destruction.

Origin

Poseidon is the son of the Titans Cronus and Rhea. He is the brother of Zeus, the king of the gods, and Hades, the god of the underworld. According to myth, after the overthrow of Cronus, the world was divided among the three brothers: Zeus took the sky, Hades the underworld, and Poseidon the sea. Poseidon's domain also includes lakes, rivers, and other bodies of water.

Lore

Poseidon's mythological tales are numerous and varied:

1. **Creation of Horses**: Poseidon is credited with the creation of horses. In some myths, he is said to have created the first horse, Skyphios, in a contest with Athena over the patronage of Athens. Although Athena won by creating the olive tree, Poseidon's connection to horses remained significant.

2. **Contest for Athens**: Poseidon competed with Athena for the city of Athens. He struck the Acropolis with his trident, creating a saltwater spring, while Athena offered an olive tree. The people of Athens chose Athena's gift, and the city was named after her, but Poseidon remained an important deity in the city.

3. **Wrath and Revenge**: Poseidon's temper is well-documented. He caused earthquakes and shipwrecks when angered. One famous tale is his involvement in the Odyssey, where he curses Odysseus to wander the seas for ten years as punishment for blinding his son, the Cyclops Polyphemus.

Additional Facts

- **Symbols and Attributes**: Poseidon's primary symbol is the trident. He is also associated with horses and dolphins. Temples dedicated to him were often located near the sea, such as the famous Temple of Poseidon at Cape Sounion.

- **Roman Equivalent**: Poseidon's counterpart in Roman mythology is Neptune, who shares similar attributes and domains.

Resources

1. Theoi Greek Mythology: A site dedicated to Greek mythology that offers detailed descriptions and references about Poseidon.

66

PROMETHEUS

(GREEK)

Description

Prometheus, a figure from Greek mythology, is a Titan known for his intelligence and for being a benefactor to humanity. He is typically depicted as a rebellious and cunning deity, often in conflict with Zeus, the king of the Olympian gods. Prometheus' name means "fore-thought," indicating his ability to plan and think ahead. He is often represented in art and literature as enduring eternal punishment for his transgressions against Zeus.

Origin

Prometheus is the son of the Titan Iapetus and the Oceanid Clymene. His siblings include Atlas, Menoetius, and Epimetheus. Unlike his fellow Titans who opposed Zeus, Prometheus sided with the Olympians during the Titanomachy, the war between the Titans and the Olympians. Despite this allegiance, his later actions led to severe punishment from Zeus.

Lore

Prometheus is best known for two significant myths:

1. **The Theft of Fire**: Prometheus is credited with stealing fire from the gods and giving it to humanity. This act of defiance enabled humans to progress and develop civilization. He concealed the fire in a hollow fennel stalk and brought it to earth, an act that enraged Zeus.

2. **Creation of Man**: In some versions of the myth, Prometheus is said to have created humans from clay. He molded them into the shape of the gods and endowed them with life, marking the beginning of human existence.

Due to his defiance, Zeus punished Prometheus by having him chained to a rock where an eagle would eat his liver daily. Being immortal, Prometheus' liver would regenerate each night, making his punishment eternal. This torment continued until Heracles (Hercules) killed the eagle and freed Prometheus as part of his Twelve Labors.

Additional Facts

- **Symbolism**: Prometheus is often viewed as a symbol of human striving and the quest for knowledge, as well as the suffering that can accompany it. He embodies the spirit of rebellion and the pursuit of enlightenment.

- **Influence in Literature**: Prometheus' story has influenced many literary works, including "Prometheus Bound" by Aeschylus and Mary Shelley's "Frankenstein," subtitled "The Modern Prometheus."

Resources

1. "Theogony" by Hesiod: This ancient text provides an account of the origins of the gods.

67

QUETZALCOATL

(LATIN AMERICAN)

Description

Quetzalcoatl, meaning "Feathered Serpent" in Nahuatl, is a prominent deity in Mesoamerican culture, particularly within the Aztec and Toltec civilizations. Depicted as a serpent adorned with feathers, Quetzalcoatl symbolizes a union of the terrestrial and the celestial. He is associated with wind, air, and learning, often portrayed with a human form wearing a conical hat, a shell necklace, and carrying a staff. The deity's iconography combines elements of a bird (quetzal) and a snake (coatl), emphasizing his dual nature as both earthbound and ethereal.

Origin

Quetzalcoatl's origins trace back to the early Mesoamerican civilizations, predating the Aztecs. He was initially venerated by the Olmec and later became central to the Toltec and Aztec pantheons. In Aztec mythology, Quetzalcoatl is considered one of the four primordial gods, born from the union of Ometeotl, the supreme dual deity. His worship spread across various Mesoamerican cultures, each adapting his mythology to their context.

Lore

The lore of Quetzalcoatl is rich and varied. In Aztec mythology, he is credited with creating humanity by sprinkling his blood on the bones of previous generations. As a god of wisdom and learning, Quetzalcoatl introduced agriculture, writing, and the calendar to humanity. A significant myth involves his rivalry with Tezcatlipoca, another powerful deity. Tezcatlipoca's trickery led to Quetzalcoatl's temporary exile. In some versions, this exile took Quetzalcoatl to the east, where he vowed to return, a legend that significantly influenced the Aztec reception of Spanish conquistadors.

Additional Facts

- **Symbolism**: Quetzalcoatl's feathered serpent form represents the integration of opposite forces, such as earth and sky, and life and death.
- **Astronomical Associations**: Quetzalcoatl is often linked with the planet Venus, symbolizing his dual role as the Morning Star and the Evening Star.

Resources

1. "The Mythology of Mexico and Central America" by John Bierhorst
2. "The Feathered Serpent: Quetzalcoatl in Mesoamerican Mythology" by Enrico A. Maurer
3. "Aztec Thought and Culture: A Study of the Ancient Nahuatl Mind" by Miguel León-Portilla

68

RA

(EGYPTIAN)

Description

Ra is one of the most important and revered deities in ancient Egyptian mythology, known as the god of the sun, creation, and kingship. Often depicted as a man with the head of a falcon, crowned with a solar disk encircled by a serpent, Ra symbolizes light, warmth, and growth. He is also depicted as a scarab beetle or a man with the head of a ram, emphasizing his connection to creation and rebirth.

Origin

Ra's origin is rooted in the early dynastic period of ancient Egypt. He emerged as a central deity in the Egyptian pantheon, eventually merging with other major gods, including Amun and Horus, to form composite deities like Amun-Ra. Ra's primary cult center was Heliopolis (the city of the sun), where he was worshipped as the creator of all life.

Lore

Ra's myths are rich with themes of creation, power, and renewal:

- **Creation Myth**: According to Egyptian mythology, Ra created himself from the primordial waters of Nun by uttering his own name. He then created Shu (air) and Tefnut (moisture), who in turn produced Geb (earth) and Nut (sky). From this lineage came Osiris, Isis, Seth, and Nephthys. Ra's act of creation established the order of the universe.

- **Eye of Ra**: The Eye of Ra is a powerful and protective force, often depicted as a separate entity in the form of a lioness, a cobra, or a vulture. It represents Ra's fierce and protective nature. The eye was sent to punish those who defied Ra's authority, and it played a crucial role in maintaining order.

Additional Facts

- **Sun Disk and Symbols**: Ra's symbols include the sun disk, the ankh (symbolizing life), and the scepter. The sun disk is often depicted encircled by a serpent, representing protection and the eternal cycle of life.

- **The Book of the Dead**: Ra plays a central role in the "Book of the Dead," guiding the deceased through the afterlife. The text includes spells and prayers to ensure safe passage and rebirth, reflecting Ra's connection to life, death, and renewal.

- **Solar Deities Across Cultures**: Ra's influence extends beyond Egypt. Similar solar deities appear in various cultures, symbolizing the universal importance of the sun in human life and spirituality.

Resources

1. "The Gods of the Egyptians" by E.A. Wallis Budge: A comprehensive study of Egyptian deities, including detailed information on Ra's mythology and worship.

69

SCYLLA

(GREEK)

Description

Scylla is a fearsome sea monster in Greek mythology, known for her terrifying appearance and her role as a maritime hazard. She is often depicted with multiple heads, each resembling a ferocious dog or a serpent, and a lower body comprised of grotesque sea creatures. Scylla inhabits one side of a narrow strait, directly opposite the whirlpool monster Charybdis, making the passage treacherous for sailors.

Origin

Scylla's origins vary in different myths, but she is typically described as a nymph transformed into a monster. In one version, she is the daughter of Phorcys and Ceto, ancient sea deities. Another version suggests she was born to Hecate, the goddess of witchcraft. The most famous transformation story involves the sea god Glaucus falling in love with Scylla. When she rejected him, he sought the help of the sorceress Circe, who, out of jealousy or spite, transformed Scylla into a monster by pouring a potion into the sea where she bathed.

Lore

Scylla's story is closely tied to her role as a perilous obstacle for sailors:

- **The Odyssey**: Scylla is prominently featured in Homer's "Odyssey." Odysseus must navigate the strait between Scylla and Charybdis. On Circe's advice, he chooses to sail closer to Scylla, accepting the inevitable loss of some of his men rather than risking the entire ship in Charybdis's whirlpool. As predicted, Scylla seizes and devours six of Odysseus's men with her multiple heads.
- **The Argonautica**: In Apollonius of Rhodes' "Argonautica," Jason and the Argonauts also face the threat of Scylla and Charybdis during their quest for the Golden Fleece. They survive the passage with the help of the sea goddess Thetis, who guides their ship.

Additional Facts

- **Dual Threat**: Scylla and Charybdis represent a classic "between a rock and a hard place" dilemma in Greek mythology, forcing sailors to choose between two deadly hazards.
- **Symbolism**: Scylla symbolizes unavoidable danger and the harsh realities of seafaring life in ancient times. Her myth highlights the themes of loss, sacrifice, and the perilous journey.

Resources

1. "The Odyssey" by Homer: Provides the most detailed account of Scylla's role in Odysseus's journey and her terrifying presence.
2. "The Argonautica" by Apollonius of Rhodes: Describes the encounter of Jason and the Argonauts with Scylla.

70

SEKHMET

(EGYPTIAN)

Description

Sekhmet is one of the most powerful and fearsome deities in ancient Egyptian mythology, known as the goddess of war, destruction, and healing. She is typically depicted as a lioness or as a woman with the head of a lioness, often crowned with a solar disk and a uraeus (a rearing cobra). Sekhmet's ferocity in battle and her protective nature make her a complex and revered figure.

Origin

Sekhmet's origins are deeply rooted in ancient Egyptian religion, particularly in the mythology surrounding the sun god Ra. She is said to be the daughter of Ra, created by him to punish humanity for their disobedience and to uphold Ma'at, the divine order. Sekhmet's name means "the powerful one," reflecting her formidable nature.

Lore

Sekhmet's myths emphasize her dual role as a bringer of both destruction and healing:

- **The Destruction of Mankind**: One of the most famous myths involving Sekhmet is her role in the "Destruction of Mankind." According to this story, Ra, angered by humanity's rebellion, sent Sekhmet to punish them. In her bloodthirsty rampage, she nearly exterminated the human race. To stop her, Ra tricked her by dyeing beer to look like blood. Sekhmet drank the beer, became intoxicated, and fell asleep, thus sparing humanity.

- **War and Healing**: Despite her destructive capabilities, Sekhmet also has a significant aspect as a healer. She was invoked for protection and healing, particularly during plagues and epidemics. This duality reflects the belief that the same divine power could cause and cure disease.

- **Patron of Physicians and Surgeons**: Sekhmet was revered by ancient Egyptian healers. Her priests were considered some of the most skilled medical practitioners, and she was often invoked during medical procedures.

Additional Facts

- **Symbolism of the Lioness**: The lioness, known for her strength and hunting prowess, symbolizes Sekhmet's fierce and protective nature. Her association with the lioness underscores her role as a guardian and warrior.

- **Solar Connections**: As the daughter of Ra, Sekhmet is closely associated with the sun. The solar disk on her head signifies her connection to the sun's life-giving and destructive powers.

Resources

1. "Egyptian Mythology: A Guide to the Gods, Goddesses, and Traditions of Ancient Egypt" by Geraldine Pinch.

71

SHAPESHIFTER

(Greek, Norse)

Description

Shapeshifters are mythical beings or creatures endowed with the ability to change their form or appearance at will. This transformative power allows them to assume the shapes of animals, other humans, or even inanimate objects. Shapeshifters are prominent in many cultures and mythologies around the world, often symbolizing themes of change, duality, and deception.

Origin

The concept of shapeshifting is ancient and widespread, appearing in various forms across different cultures. In many traditions, shapeshifters are depicted as gods, spirits, or magical beings who possess the innate ability to alter their form. The origins of these myths often reflect humanity's fascination with transformation and the blurred boundaries between the natural and supernatural worlds.

Lore

Shapeshifters appear in numerous myths and legends, with each culture adding unique elements to their stories:

- **Greek Mythology**: In Greek mythology, Proteus is an early example of a shapeshifter. Known as the "Old Man of the Sea," Proteus could change his form at will and was often sought after for his ability to foretell the future. Another famous shapeshifter is Zeus, who frequently transformed himself to pursue his romantic interests.

- **Norse Mythology**: Loki, the trickster god, is renowned for his shapeshifting abilities. Loki could transform into various animals and human forms, using his powers for both mischief and strategic advantage. In one myth, he turns into a mare to distract a giant's stallion, leading to the birth of Sleipnir, Odin's eight-legged horse.

- **American Indian Mythology**: Many Native American tribes have legends of shapeshifters, often involving animal spirits. The Navajo skinwalker, for example, is a witch who can transform into any animal to cause harm or mischief. In contrast, other tribes have benevolent shapeshifters, such as the Anishinaabe's hero Nanabozho, who uses his abilities to teach and guide.

Additional Facts

- **Symbolism of Duality**: Shapeshifters often symbolize duality and the fluid nature of identity. Their ability to change form reflects the complex and multifaceted nature of beings and the world around them.

- **Shamanic Practices**: In many indigenous cultures, shamans are believed to possess the ability to shapeshift. This spiritual transformation is often used for healing, protection, and communication with the spirit world.

Resources

"The Odyssey" by Homer: Contains stories of Proteus, the shape-shifting sea god.

72

SHIVA

(HINDU)

Description

Shiva, one of the principal deities in Hinduism, is widely revered as the "Destroyer" within the Trimurti, the trinity of gods that includes Brahma (the creator) and Vishnu (the preserver). However, Shiva's role extends beyond mere destruction—he is also associated with regeneration and transformation, embodying the cycle of creation, destruction, and rebirth that is central to the universe's existence.

Shiva is often depicted as a powerful ascetic, sitting in meditation with a serene expression, his body covered in ash to signify his connection to cremation grounds. He has matted hair, from which the sacred river Ganges flows, symbolizing life-giving purity. Around his neck, Shiva wears a snake, and a crescent moon rests on his head. His third eye, in the center of his forehead, signifies his ability to see beyond the material world, representing wisdom and destruction of evil. The Trishula (trident), a symbol of his power, is almost always by his side.

Origin

Shiva's origins are ancient and complex, rooted in Vedic traditions, Dravidian beliefs, and later developments in Hinduism. In the early Vedic texts, he is identified with **Rudra**, a storm god associated with hunting and wildness, later evolving into the more benevolent and complex figure of Shiva.

Lore

Shiva's stories are rich in symbolism and profound teachings. One of the most famous myths involves the **Churning of the Ocean (Samudra Manthan)**, where Shiva drinks the poison **Halahala** to save the universe, turning his throat blue in the process. Hence, he is also known as **Neelkanth** ("The Blue-Throated One").

Another key myth centers around his marriage to **Parvati**, the goddess of fertility, love, and devotion. This union represents the balance between the forces of destruction and creation. Together, they have two sons: **Ganesha**, the elephant-headed god of wisdom and new beginnings, and **Kartikeya**, the god of war.

Additional Facts:

- **Ardhanarishvara**: One unique depiction of Shiva is in the form of **Ardhanarishvara**, where his body is split into half-male and half-female, symbolizing the union of opposites—Shiva and Parvati, or male and female, representing cosmic balance and the interdependence of energies.

- **Shiva's Consort and Family**: Shiva's wife, Parvati, takes on various forms, including **Durga**, the warrior goddess, and **Kali**, the fierce destroyer of evil. Their son, Ganesha, is worshipped across India as the remover of obstacles and lord of new beginnings. Kartikeya, another son, is widely revered in southern India as a god of war and protector of dharma.

- **Shiva's Role in Yoga**: As the first yogi or **Adiyogi**, Shiva is considered the originator of the yogic tradition. Many schools of yoga trace their spiritual roots to the teachings and practices of Shiva. He is seen as the master of asceticism and meditation.

Resources

1. **The Shiva Purana** – One of the major Puranic texts dedicated to the lore, mythology, and worship of Shiva.

2. **"Shiva: Stories and Teachings from the Shiva Mahapurana" by Vanamali.**

73

SIREN

(GREEK)

Description

Sirens are mythical creatures in Greek mythology, known for their enchanting music and singing voices that lured sailors to their doom. Traditionally depicted as part woman and part bird, later depictions in medieval and modern art often portray them as beautiful women with fish tails, similar to mermaids. Sirens symbolize both temptation and the perilous allure of beauty.

Origin

The Sirens are believed to be the daughters of the river god Achelous and one of the Muses, either Melpomene, Calliope, or Terpsichore, according to various myths. Their origin is tied to the sea and the idea of dangerous beauty, reflecting the Greeks' understanding of the perilous and unpredictable nature of the ocean.

Lore

The Sirens' most famous myths involve their encounters with famous Greek heroes:

- **The Odyssey**: In Homer's "Odyssey," Odysseus encounters the Sirens during his journey home from the Trojan War. Forewarned about their enchanting song, Odysseus orders his men to plug their ears with beeswax and ties himself to the mast of his ship so he can listen to their singing without succumbing to their lure. This encounter emphasizes the themes of temptation and self-control.
- **Argonautica**: In Apollonius of Rhodes' "Argonautica," the hero Jason and the Argonauts also encounter the Sirens. They are saved by Orpheus, whose music is more beautiful and drowns out the Sirens' song, allowing the crew to pass safely. This story highlights the power of art and beauty to overcome danger.

Additional Facts

- **Symbolism of Temptation**: Sirens are often seen as symbols of temptation and the dangerous allure of the unknown. Their ability to enchant and destroy reflects the human struggle with desires and the consequences of succumbing to them.
- **Etymology**: The term "siren" has entered the modern lexicon to describe anything that is alluring yet potentially dangerous. The word is used in contexts ranging from the "siren song" of temptation to the loud, attention-grabbing sirens of emergency vehicles.

Resources

1. "The Odyssey" by Homer: Provides one of the earliest and most famous accounts of the Sirens, highlighting their role in Odysseus's journey.

74

SLEIPNIR

(NORSE)

Description

Sleipnir is a prominent figure in Norse mythology, known as the eight-legged horse of the god Odin. Sleipnir is renowned for his speed and strength, often described as the best of all horses, capable of traveling between the worlds of the living and the dead. His eight legs make him incredibly swift and stable, enabling him to traverse great distances with ease.

Origin

Sleipnir's origin is unique and intertwined with Loki's mischief. According to the "Prose Edda" by Snorri Sturluson, Sleipnir was born from Loki, who had transformed himself into a mare. This transformation was part of a scheme to distract the stallion Svadilfari, owned by a giant tasked with building a fortress for the gods. Loki, as a mare, lured Svadilfari away, resulting in the giant failing to complete his task on time. From this union, Sleipnir was born, and he was later given to Odin.

Lore

Sleipnir's stories are rich with symbolism and connections to various myths:

- **Odin's Steed**: As Odin's trusted steed, Sleipnir plays a crucial role in many myths. He is capable of traveling between the realms of Asgard (home of the gods), Midgard (earth), and Hel (the underworld). Sleipnir's ability to navigate these worlds makes him invaluable to Odin, particularly in his role as a psychopomp, guiding souls to the afterlife.

- **Journey to Hel**: In one famous myth, Odin rides Sleipnir to the underworld to consult the dead seeress for knowledge about the fate of his son, Baldr. This journey highlights Sleipnir's extraordinary abilities and his role in bridging the worlds of the living and the dead.

Additional Facts

- **Unique Birth**: Sleipnir's birth from Loki, who transformed into a mare, adds an element of trickery and transformation to his origin story. This unusual birth highlights the fluidity and complexity of Norse myths.

- **Connection to Yggdrasil**: Sleipnir is sometimes associated with Yggdrasil, the World Tree, which connects all the realms in Norse cosmology. His ability to travel between realms parallels the tree's function as a cosmic connector.

- **Sleipnir and Shamanic Practices**: Some scholars suggest that Sleipnir's ability to travel between worlds may be linked to shamanic practices, where shamans would undertake spiritual journeys to other realms, often accompanied by spirit animals.

Resources

1. "Prose Edda" by Snorri Sturluson: Provides detailed accounts of Sleipnir's origin and his role in Norse mythology.

75

SPHINX

(Egyptian, Greek)

Description

The Sphinx is a mythical creature with the body of a lion and the head of a human. Often depicted as a male in Egyptian mythology and as a female in Greek mythology, the Sphinx symbolizes wisdom, strength, and mystery. The Egyptian Sphinx is typically portrayed with a calm and majestic expression, while the Greek Sphinx is more menacing and enigmatic. This creature combines the physical prowess of a lion with the intelligence of a human, making it a formidable guardian and symbol of riddles and knowledge.

Origin

The concept of the Sphinx has origins in both Egyptian and Greek mythology, each with distinct characteristics and stories. The earliest representations of the Sphinx are found in ancient Egypt, where it was associated with the sun god Ra and believed to protect sacred sites. The Great Sphinx of Giza, dating back to around 2500 BCE, is one of the most iconic and enduring symbols of ancient Egypt.

In Greek mythology, the Sphinx is known for its role in the legend of Oedipus. This version of the Sphinx, described as a female monster with the body of a lion, the wings of an eagle, and the face of a woman, posed a deadly riddle to travelers and devoured those who could not solve it.

Lore

The Egyptian Sphinx was seen as a benevolent guardian, protecting temples and tombs from evil forces. It was often depicted as a male with a pharaoh's headdress, emphasizing its role as a protector of the divine and the royal. The Great Sphinx of Giza, located near the pyramids, is one of the largest and oldest statues in the world, symbolizing the power and wisdom of the pharaohs.

In Greek mythology, the Sphinx is infamous for its riddle: "What walks on four legs in the morning, two legs at noon, and three legs in the evening?" The answer, "Man," refers to the stages of human life—crawling as a baby, walking on two legs as an adult, and using a cane in old age. Oedipus famously solved the riddle, leading to the Sphinx's demise. This tale highlights the themes of human intelligence, fate, and the consequences of knowledge.

Additional Facts

- **Symbolism:** The Sphinx represents a blend of human intelligence and animal strength. It is a symbol of protection, wisdom, and the enduring power of mysteries and riddles.
- **Cultural Significance:** The Sphinx has been a prominent figure in art, literature, and architecture across different cultures. It embodies the convergence of human and divine, earthly and spiritual realms.
- **Literary References:** The Sphinx appears in various works of literature, from the ancient Greek tragedies of Sophocles to modern adaptations in novels and films.

Resources

1. "Mythology: Timeless Tales of Gods and Heroes" by Edith Hamilton: Provides detailed accounts of Greek myths, including the story of the Sphinx and Oedipus.
2. "The Complete Gods and Goddesses of Ancient Egypt" by Richard H. Wilkinson: Explores the mythology and significance of Egyptian deities, including the Sphinx.

76

THOR

(NORSE)

Description

Thor is one of the most prominent deities in Norse mythology, known as the god of thunder, lightning, storms, oak trees, strength, the protection of mankind, and also hallowing and fertility. He is typically depicted as a powerful, red-bearded man wielding the mighty hammer Mjölnir, which has the power to destroy mountains and defeat giants. Thor's formidable presence and martial prowess make him a central figure in Norse myth and folklore.

Origin

Thor is the son of Odin, the chief of the gods, and Jord (also known as Fjörgyn), the personification of the Earth. He belongs to the Aesir, one of the principal groups of gods in Norse mythology. His Roman equivalent is Jupiter, the god of sky and thunder, reflecting the shared Indo-European heritage of these mythological traditions.

Lore

Thor's adventures and exploits are central to many Norse myths, often highlighting themes of heroism, strength, and the battle against chaos:

- **Mjölnir**: Thor's hammer, Mjölnir, is his most iconic weapon. It is said to always return to his hand after being thrown and is capable of leveling mountains. Mjölnir is also used to bless events, such as weddings and births, and to consecrate objects.

- **Ragnarök**: Thor is destined to play a crucial role in Ragnarök, the prophesied end of the world. He will fight the Midgard Serpent, and though he will slay the beast, he will succumb to its venom shortly after. His death marks the fall of the old world and the dawn of a new era.

Additional Facts

- **Symbol of Protection**: Thor is often invoked for protection and strength. His hammer, Mjölnir, is a common symbol worn as an amulet for protection against evil.

- **The Day of Thor**: Thursday ("Thor's day") is named after him, indicating his influence on the modern calendar and the enduring legacy of his myth.

Resources

1. "The Poetic Edda": A collection of Old Norse poems that provide insights into Thor's myths and his role in Norse mythology.

2. "Norse Mythology" by Neil Gaiman: A modern retelling of Norse myths, including stories about Thor.

77

THUNDERBIRD

(American Indian)

Description

The Thunderbird is a powerful and mythical creature in the folklore of various Indigenous cultures across North America. It is often depicted as a gigantic bird with supernatural strength and abilities, particularly the power to create thunder and lightning. The Thunderbird symbolizes power, protection, and is considered a guardian of the natural world.

Origin

The concept of the Thunderbird varies among different Indigenous tribes, but it is generally viewed as a divine entity. The origin stories of the Thunderbird are rich and diverse, reflecting the cultural significance and reverence it holds in various traditions. Among the Algonquian-speaking peoples, the Thunderbird is a prominent figure, as it is among the Plains tribes, including the Lakota, Dakota, and Sioux.

Lore

The Thunderbird's lore is rich with themes of power, protection, and natural forces:

- **Creation of Thunder and Lightning**: The Thunderbird is believed to create thunder by flapping its enormous wings and lightning by flashing its eyes. Storms are often seen as the manifestation of the Thunderbird's anger or its battle with other mythical creatures.

- **Battles with Water Spirits**: A common motif involves the Thunderbird engaging in epic battles with water spirits or serpents, such as the Underwater Panthers or the Horned Serpents. These battles symbolize the struggle between the forces of the sky and water, often resulting in storms and natural disturbances.

Additional Facts

- **Symbolism of Power**: The Thunderbird's immense size and strength symbolize the power and majesty of nature. Its ability to control the weather reflects the deep connection between the natural world and the spiritual beliefs of Indigenous cultures.

- **Sacred Animal**: The Thunderbird is considered a sacred animal and is often depicted in art, including pottery, basketry, and carvings. It is also a central figure in ceremonial dances and rituals.

Resources

1. "The Encyclopedia of Native American Religions" by Arlene Hirschfelder and Paulette Molin: Provides detailed information on the spiritual beliefs and practices of various Indigenous cultures, including the Thunderbird.

78

THUNDER CHILDREN

(American Indian)

Description

Thunder children are mythological figures found in various cultures around the world, typically embodying the power and might of thunderstorms. They are often depicted as children or young beings with control over thunder and lightning, embodying the raw energy and untamed nature of these phenomena. These mythological figures are sometimes associated with deities of thunder and lightning or considered their offspring.

Origin

The concept of thunder children appears in several cultural mythologies, each with unique characteristics and lore:

1. **Navajo Mythology**: Among the Navajo people, there is a belief in the "Thunder Twins," who are considered the children of the Sun God and the Goddess of the Earth. These twins are associated with the natural elements and are believed to control thunder and lightning, playing a role in the Navajo creation stories and natural world phenomena.

2. **Asian Mythology**: In Japanese mythology, Raijin, the god of thunder and lightning, is sometimes depicted with children who assist him in creating thunderstorms. These children are often mischievous and playful, reflecting the unpredictable nature of storms.

Lore

The lore surrounding thunder children varies widely depending on the cultural context. Common themes include:

- **Birth During Storms**: Many myths describe thunder children as being born during intense thunderstorms, with the thunder and lightning marking their arrival. These children are often seen as omens or signs of significant events.

- **Powers and Abilities**: Thunder children are typically depicted with the ability to control or summon thunder and lightning. In some stories, they can also influence weather patterns, bringing rain or storms to their communities.

Additional Facts

- **Protective Roles**: In some cultures, thunder children are seen as protectors, using their powers to ward off evil spirits or enemies. Their presence is believed to bring strength and protection to their communities.

Resources

1. "The Navajo" by Peter Iverson: A comprehensive look at Navajo culture and mythology, including the story of the Thunder Twins.

79

TROLL

(EUROPEAN)

Description

Trolls are mythical creatures found primarily in Norse and Scandinavian folklore. They are often depicted as large, brutish beings with a fearsome appearance, though their size and characteristics can vary. Trolls are typically associated with nature, particularly mountains, forests, and caves, and are known for their hostility towards humans. They embody themes of wilderness, primal strength, and the untamed aspects of nature.

Origin

The concept of trolls originates from Norse mythology and Scandinavian folklore. The word "troll" comes from Old Norse "troll" or "trold," which can mean giant, monster, or supernatural being. Trolls were believed to inhabit remote, rugged landscapes, far from human civilization. Their myths have been passed down through generations in the form of sagas, folklore, and fairy tales.

Lore

Trolls appear in various myths and legends, each culture adding unique attributes and stories:

- **Norse Mythology**: In Norse mythology, trolls are often depicted as Jotnar (giants) and are considered ancient enemies of the gods, particularly the Aesir. They are associated with chaos and destruction, opposing the order established by the gods. Trolls in Norse myths are usually depicted as massive, powerful beings with an elemental connection to the earth.
- **Scandinavian Folklore**: In Scandinavian folklore, trolls are more diverse in appearance and behavior. They can range from being monstrous and evil to more benign and even comical. They are often described as living in mountains, forests, or caves, and they turn to stone if exposed to sunlight. This vulnerability to sunlight is a common theme, symbolizing the triumph of day (order) over night (chaos).

Additional Facts

- **Trolls and Nature**: Trolls are closely tied to nature and are often seen as its guardians. They are associated with natural formations, such as mountains and rock formations, which were sometimes believed to be trolls turned to stone by the sun.
- **Symbolism of Trolls**: Trolls symbolize the wild, untamed aspects of nature and the primal fears of the unknown. Their resistance to sunlight represents the victory of light (order) over darkness (chaos).

Resources

1. "Norse Mythology" by Neil Gaiman: A modern retelling of Norse myths, including stories of giants and trolls.
2. "The Prose Edda" by Snorri Sturluson: An essential source for Norse mythology.

80

TYR

(NORSE)

Description

Tyr is a prominent god in Norse mythology, known for his association with law, justice, and heroic glory. Often depicted as a one-handed warrior, Tyr embodies the principles of honor, bravery, and sacrifice. His name is derived from the Proto-Germanic "*Tiwaz*" and is cognate with the Old English "*Tiw*" and Old High German "*Ziu*."

Origin

Tyr is one of the oldest deities in the Norse pantheon and originally held a higher position among the gods, possibly even as the chief deity before being supplanted by Odin. He is the son of Odin or, in some accounts, the giant Hymir. Tyr's Roman equivalent is Mars, the god of war, reflecting his martial attributes.

Lore

Tyr's most famous myth involves the binding of the wolf Fenrir, highlighting his role as a god of law and his willingness to sacrifice for the greater good:

- **The Binding of Fenrir**: Fenrir, a monstrous wolf and one of Loki's offspring, was prophesied to bring great destruction. The gods decided to bind him to prevent this fate. Fenrir agreed to be bound only if one of the gods placed their hand in his mouth as a sign of good faith. Tyr, known for his bravery and integrity, volunteered and placed his right hand in Fenrir's mouth. When Fenrir realized he had been tricked and could not break free, he bit off Tyr's hand. This act of sacrifice secured Tyr's reputation as a god of justice and valor.

- **Ragnarök**: During the prophesied end of the world, Ragnarök, Tyr is destined to face Garm, the monstrous hound guarding Hel's realm. Both Tyr and Garm are fated to die in the encounter, symbolizing the ultimate sacrifice for the restoration of cosmic order.

Additional Facts

- **Symbol of Justice:** Tyr's association with law and justice is reflected in his willingness to sacrifice his hand to uphold a binding agreement. He is often invoked in matters of legal disputes and oaths.

- **Tyr's Day**: Tuesday is named after Tyr (from Old English "Tiwesdæg"), indicating his significant influence on the modern calendar and his enduring legacy.

Resources

1. "The Poetic Edda": A collection of Old Norse poems that provide insights into Tyr's myths and his

81

UNICORN

(GREEK)

Description

Unicorns are legendary creatures known for their beauty, grace, and mystical qualities. Typically depicted as a white horse with a single spiraling horn on its forehead, the unicorn symbolizes purity, innocence, and magical power. The horn, often referred to as the alicorn, is believed to possess healing properties and the ability to neutralize poison.

Origin

The concept of the unicorn dates back to ancient civilizations, with early mentions found in Mesopotamian art and references in ancient Indian and Chinese texts. The Greeks and Romans also wrote about unicorns, describing them as wild animals from distant lands like India. These early descriptions contributed to the unicorn's enduring presence in folklore and mythology.

Lore

Unicorns have appeared in various myths and legends throughout history, often embodying themes of purity, magic, and elusive beauty:

- **Medieval European Lore**: In medieval Europe, unicorns were often depicted as woodland creatures that could only be tamed by a virgin maiden. This association with purity and innocence reinforced their symbolic connection to chastity and grace. Unicorns became a popular subject in medieval tapestries and literature, often representing Christ and divine truth.
- **Healing Properties**: The unicorn's horn, or alicorn, was believed to have powerful medicinal properties. It was said to cure diseases, neutralize poisons, and purify water. This belief persisted into the Renaissance, where unicorn horn powder was highly prized and sold at high prices.
- **Eastern Mythology**: In Chinese mythology, a similar creature called the Qilin is considered a symbol of good fortune and prosperity. The Qilin, often depicted with a single horn, is said to appear during times of peace and prosperity and is associated with the birth of great sages and rulers.

Additional Facts

- **Symbolism of Purity**: Unicorns are universally recognized as symbols of purity, innocence, and unblemished beauty. This symbolism extends to their depiction in art, literature, and heraldry.
- **Heraldic Emblems**: Unicorns were used in heraldry during the Middle Ages, symbolizing strength, purity, and protection. The unicorn is a prominent element in the royal coat of arms of Scotland and later the United Kingdom.

Resources

1. "The Lore of the Unicorn" by Odell Shepard: A comprehensive exploration of unicorn mythology.

82

URANUS

(GREEK)

Description

Uranus, also known as Ouranos, is a primordial deity in Greek mythology, representing the sky. He is often depicted as the embodiment of the heavens, sometimes portrayed as a starry sky or a majestic figure reclining across the sky. Uranus is a fundamental figure in Greek cosmogony, symbolizing the vast and encompassing nature of the heavens.

Origin

Uranus is one of the first gods, born from Gaia (the Earth) without a consort. In some versions of the myth, he is also considered a son of Aether (the upper sky) and Hemera (the day). Uranus and Gaia together represent the union of the sky and the earth, a common theme in many mythologies.

Lore

Uranus's story is deeply intertwined with themes of creation, power, and the cyclical nature of time:

- **Union with Gaia**: Uranus and Gaia together produced many offspring, known as the Titans, the Cyclopes, and the Hecatoncheires (hundred-handed ones). Uranus's fear of being overthrown by his powerful children led him to imprison them within Gaia, causing her great pain.
- **Overthrow by Cronus**: Distressed by Uranus's actions, Gaia conspired with her youngest Titan son, Cronus. She provided Cronus with a sickle, and when Uranus came to lie with Gaia, Cronus ambushed him and castrated him. The blood from Uranus fell onto Gaia, giving rise to the Erinyes (Furies), the Giants, and the Meliae (ash tree nymphs). His severed genitals fell into the sea, and from the sea foam emerged Aphrodite, the goddess of love and beauty.
- **Succession and Legacy**: After Uranus was overthrown, Cronus became the ruler of the cosmos, only to be later overthrown by his own son, Zeus, continuing the cycle of succession and power struggles among the gods.

Additional Facts

- **Symbolism of the Sky**: Uranus's domain over the sky symbolizes the vastness and omnipresence of the heavens. His story reflects the natural order and the cyclical nature of creation and destruction.
- **Etymology**: The name "Uranus" has been used in modern times to name the seventh planet from the Sun, discovered in 1781. This naming continues the tradition of using Greek mythology to name celestial bodies.

Resources

1. "Greek Religion" by Walter Burkert: Explores the broader context of Greek religious beliefs and practices.

83

VALKYRIE

(NORSE)

Description

Valkyries are powerful and ethereal warrior maidens from Norse mythology, often depicted as beautiful, fierce, and formidable figures. They are known for their radiant beauty, flowing hair, and warrior attire, which includes armor and weapons like spears and shields. Valkyries possess an aura of divine authority and are often shown riding winged horses or wolves, soaring over battlefields with grace and strength.

Origin

The concept of Valkyries originates from Norse mythology, particularly from the sagas and Eddas composed in medieval Scandinavia. The word "Valkyrie" comes from the Old Norse term "valkyrja," meaning "chooser of the slain." These mythological figures are closely associated with Odin, the chief of the gods, who entrusts them with selecting the bravest warriors slain in battle and guiding them to Valhalla, the hall of the slain.

Lore

Valkyries play a crucial role in the afterlife beliefs of Norse culture. They are sent by Odin to the battlefields to choose the fallen warriors worthy of Valhalla. These chosen warriors, known as Einherjar, are brought to Valhalla, where they prepare for Ragnarok, the prophesied end of the world. In Valhalla, the warriors engage in daily battles to hone their skills and feast with the gods at night.

Valkyries are also seen as protectors and guides for these warriors. They ensure that the bravest and most honorable warriors receive their due rewards in the afterlife. Valkyries can be both benevolent and terrifying, embodying the dual nature of war and fate.

Additional Facts

- **Roles and Abilities:** Valkyries have the power to influence battles, determining the fates of warriors. They can grant victory or doom to those they favor or despise. They possess magical abilities, including shape-shifting and prophecy.
- **Cultural Significance:** Valkyries symbolize the ideals of bravery, honor, and the warrior spirit. They reflect the Norse belief in the glory of a heroic death and the importance of valor in battle.
- **Literary References:** Valkyries feature prominently in various Norse sagas and Eddas. The "Poetic Edda" and the "Prose Edda," compiled by Snorri Sturluson, provide detailed accounts of Valkyries and their roles.
- **Modern Interpretations:** Valkyries have been adapted into various forms of modern media, including literature, films, and video games. They are often depicted as strong, independent female warriors, embodying themes of empowerment and heroism.

Resources

1. "The Poetic Edda" translated by Carolyne Larrington: A collection of Old Norse poems that includes tales of Valkyries and other mythological beings.

2. "The Prose Edda" by Snorri Sturluson: A key source of Norse mythology.

84

VAMPIRE

(European)

Description

Vampires are mythological beings typically described as reanimated corpses that sustain themselves by drinking the blood of the living. They are often depicted with a variety of supernatural abilities, such as immortality, enhanced strength, shapeshifting, and mind control. Vampires are usually portrayed as nocturnal creatures, vulnerable to sunlight, and possessing fangs used to puncture the skin of their victims.

Origin

The concept of vampires has roots in ancient civilizations and has evolved through folklore, literature, and popular culture. Early references to vampire-like creatures can be found in Mesopotamian, Greek, and Roman mythology. For example, the Greek "lamia" was a demon that feasted on the blood of children, and the Roman "striges" were bird-like creatures that sucked the blood of the living.

The modern image of the vampire, however, is primarily derived from Eastern European folklore. During the 18th century, there were numerous reports of vampire sightings in the Balkans and Eastern Europe, which led to widespread hysteria and vampire hunts. These tales were fueled by superstitions and the lack of scientific understanding of decomposition and diseases.

Lore

Vampire lore varies across cultures, but several common themes and characteristics emerge:

- **Transformation**: Humans could become vampires through various means, such as being bitten by a vampire, practicing witchcraft, committing suicide, or having improper burial rites.
- **Weaknesses**: Vampires have several traditional weaknesses, including sunlight, garlic, holy water, crucifixes, and wooden stakes through the heart.
- **Powers**: Vampires possess various supernatural abilities, such as immortality, enhanced physical attributes, shapeshifting (often into bats, wolves, or mist), mind control, and healing powers.

Additional Facts

Historical Accounts: During the 18th century, Europe experienced a vampire hysteria, with many people being accused of vampirism and subsequently executed. These cases were often based on superstitions and misunderstandings of natural decomposition processes.
Regional Variations: Different cultures have unique versions of vampire myths. In China, the "jiangshi" are reanimated corpses that drain the life force of the living. In India, the "vetala" are spirits that inhabit corpses and can possess the living.

Resources

1. "The Vampire: A New History" by Nick Groom.

85

VISHNU

(HINDU)

Description

Vishnu is one of the principal deities of Hinduism, known as the Preserver and Protector of the universe. He is often depicted with a dark or blue complexion, symbolizing the infinite and all-encompassing nature of the cosmos. Vishnu is usually portrayed with four arms holding a conch shell (Shankha), a discus (Chakra), a mace (Gada), and a lotus flower (Padma), each representing different aspects of his divine nature. He is also commonly shown reclining on the serpent Ananta Shesha, floating in the cosmic ocean.

Origin

Vishnu's origins are ancient, tracing back to the Vedic period, where he is mentioned in the Rigveda. Over time, his prominence grew, and he became a central figure in various Hindu traditions, particularly Vaishnavism, which focuses on the worship of Vishnu and his avatars. He is part of the Hindu trinity (Trimurti), alongside Brahma, the creator, and Shiva, the destroyer.

Lore

Vishnu's lore is rich with stories of his avatars, each of whom descends to the mortal realm to restore dharma (cosmic order) and vanquish evil:

- **Dashavatara**: Vishnu is best known for his ten principal avatars, known as the Dashavatara. rst two being:
- **The Cosmic Serpent**: Vishnu is often depicted reclining on Ananta Shesha, the cosmic serpent. This symbolizes his role in maintaining the universe and the endless cycles of creation and destruction.
- **Vishnu and Lakshmi**: Vishnu's consort is Lakshmi, the goddess of wealth and prosperity. Together, they represent the harmonious balance of cosmic energies.

Additional Facts

- **Symbolism**: Each of Vishnu's attributes symbolizes different aspects of his power. The conch represents the primordial sound "Om," the discus signifies the mind and cosmic order, the mace symbolizes strength and power, and the lotus represents purity and spiritual enlightenment.
- **Bhagavad Gita**: One of the most important texts in Hinduism, the Bhagavad Gita, is a dialogue between Krishna (an avatar of Vishnu) and the prince Arjuna, offering profound spiritual and philosophical guidance.

Resources

1. "The Bhagavad Gita": Provides essential teachings attributed to Krishna, an avatar of Vishnu, and offers insights into his philosophical and spiritual principles.

86

WEREWOLF

(European)

Description

Werewolves, also known as lycanthropes, are mythological creatures characterized by their ability to transform from human to wolf. The transformation is often depicted as occurring during the full moon, where the human undergoes a painful and dramatic metamorphosis into a wolf or a hybrid wolf-human form. Werewolves are typically portrayed as having superhuman strength, heightened senses, and a primal, often uncontrollable, rage.

Origin

The concept of the werewolf has ancient roots, with various versions appearing in the folklore of many cultures worldwide. The term "lycanthropy" comes from the Greek words "lykos" (wolf) and "anthropos" (man). The earliest references to werewolves date back to ancient Greek and Roman mythology. One of the most famous tales involves King Lycaon of Arcadia, who was transformed into a wolf by Zeus as punishment for his impiety.

In medieval Europe, werewolf legends were widespread. These stories were often associated with witchcraft and heresy, and alleged werewolves were frequently subjects of witch trials. The transformation into a werewolf was often attributed to magical spells, curses, or the wearing of enchanted items like a wolf belt or pelt.

Lore

Werewolf lore varies greatly across cultures and time periods, but several common themes emerge:

- **Transformation**: The transformation is usually triggered by the full moon, but in some legends, it can occur at will or be induced by wearing a magical item.
- **Weaknesses**: Werewolves are often vulnerable to silver weapons, a trait popularized by modern fiction. Other weaknesses include wolfsbane and holy artifacts.
- **Cure**: Methods to cure or kill a werewolf vary, including the removal of the curse through magical means, death by silver weapon, or the wolf's pelt being destroyed.

Additional Facts

- **Regional Variations**: Different cultures have unique versions of werewolf myths. For example, in Norse mythology, the saga of the Volsungs describes men who transform into wolves using enchanted wolf skins. In French folklore, the "loup-garou" is a werewolf that can be either a cursed individual or a witch in disguise.

Resources

- "The Book of Werewolves" by Sabine Baring-Gould.

87

WITCH (SORCERESS)

(EUROPEAN)

Description

Witches are mythical figures known for their magical abilities, often associated with the practice of witchcraft and sorcery. They are typically depicted as women, though male witches (warlocks or wizards) also appear in folklore. Witches are often portrayed with a variety of attributes, such as casting spells, brewing potions, flying on broomsticks, and communicating with spirits. They embody themes of power, mystery, and often danger.

Origin

The concept of witches has ancient roots, tracing back to various cultures and civilizations. The term "witch" comes from the Old English word "wicce," meaning "wise woman." Witches have been part of folklore and mythology in cultures worldwide, including ancient Greece, Rome, and Egypt. Over time, their depiction has evolved, influenced by historical, religious, and social contexts.

Lore

Witches appear in numerous myths, legends, and folklore, each culture adding unique characteristics and stories:

- **Medieval European Folklore**: During the Middle Ages, witches were often viewed with suspicion and fear. They were believed to have made pacts with the devil, granting them supernatural powers in exchange for their souls. This period saw the rise of witch hunts and trials, particularly in Europe and colonial America, where many were accused and persecuted.

- **Fairy Tales and Folklore**: Witches frequently appear in fairy tales and folklore, often as antagonists or wise women. Examples include the evil witch in "Hansel and Gretel," who lures children to her gingerbread house, and the benevolent witch in "Baba Yaga," a Slavic folklore character who can be both a helper and a hindrance to those who seek her out.

Additional Facts

- **Symbols and Tools**: Witches are often depicted with various symbols and tools, such as broomsticks, cauldrons, wands, and familiars (animal companions believed to assist in magic).

- **Witches and Nature**: Many myths and legends connect witches to nature, portraying them as guardians of ancient wisdom and herbal knowledge. They are often seen as healers who use their knowledge of plants and the natural world for both benevolent and malevolent purposes.

Resources

1. "The Witchcraft Reader" edited by Darren Oldridge: A comprehensive collection of historical texts and modern interpretations on the subject of witchcraft.

88

ZEUS

(GREEK)

Description

Zeus is the king of the gods in Greek mythology, ruling over Mount Olympus and presiding over the sky and thunder. Often depicted as a regal, bearded man wielding a thunderbolt, Zeus embodies authority, power, and justice. He is a central figure in many myths, known for his numerous affairs and resulting offspring, who play significant roles in various stories.

Origin

Zeus is the youngest son of the Titans Cronus and Rhea. According to myth, Cronus, fearing a prophecy that one of his children would overthrow him, swallowed his offspring at birth. Rhea, determined to save her youngest child, Zeus, hid him on the island of Crete and gave Cronus a stone wrapped in swaddling clothes, which he swallowed instead. Zeus grew up in secret, and upon reaching adulthood, he led a rebellion against Cronus, ultimately freeing his siblings and establishing himself as the supreme ruler of the gods.

Lore

Zeus's myths are rich with themes of power, justice, and intrigue:

- **The Titanomachy**: Zeus's rise to power involved a ten-year war known as the Titanomachy, where he and his siblings, the Olympians, fought against the Titans. With the help of the Cyclopes and the Hecatoncheires, whom Zeus freed from Tartarus, the Olympians triumphed, and Zeus became the ruler of the sky, while his brothers Poseidon and Hades ruled the sea and the underworld, respectively.

- **Marriage to Hera**: Zeus's wife is Hera, the queen of the gods, who is also his sister. Their marriage is often tumultuous due to Zeus's numerous infidelities, leading to many myths involving Hera's jealousy and vengeance.

- **The Pantheon**: As the king of the gods, Zeus presides over the Olympian pantheon, which includes gods and goddesses such as Athena, Apollo, Artemis, Hermes, Hera, Demeter, and Aphrodite. He is often called upon to settle disputes among the gods and to enforce divine justice.

Additional Facts

- **Symbols and Attributes**: Zeus's primary symbols include the thunderbolt, eagle, bull, and oak tree. The thunderbolt represents his power over the sky and weather, while the eagle symbolizes his role as a ruler and enforcer of justice.

- **Oracle of Dodona**: One of the oldest and most important oracles dedicated to Zeus was located at Dodona. Here, priests and priestesses interpreted the rustling of the leaves of the sacred oak tree to deliver divine messages.

Resources

1. "The Iliad" and "The Odyssey" by Homer: Epic poems that depict Zeus's influence over gods and mortals.

2. "The Library" by Apollodorus: A comprehensive source of Greek myths, including the stories of Zeus.

89

ZHU RONG

(CHINESE)

Description

Zhu Rong is a deity in Chinese mythology, known as the god of fire and the South. He is often depicted as a powerful figure with a fiery countenance, sometimes riding a tiger and wielding a fire-spear or staff. Zhu Rong is revered for his control over fire, which is both a destructive force and a symbol of purification and transformation.

Origin

Zhu Rong's origins are rooted in ancient Chinese mythology, where he is considered one of the important figures in the pantheon of gods. He is sometimes described as a descendant of the legendary emperor Yan Di, or as the son of Gao Yang (Emperor Zhuanxu), one of the Five Emperors. His association with fire links him to the element's crucial role in agriculture, metallurgy, and daily life in ancient China.

Lore

Zhu Rong's myths and legends often revolve around his role as the enforcer of celestial order and his battles against chaos and disorder:

- **Battle Against Gong Gong**: One of the most famous myths involving Zhu Rong is his battle against Gong Gong, the god of water, who attempted to overthrow the heavenly order. Gong Gong caused great floods and chaos in his rebellion. Zhu Rong, as the god of fire, confronted Gong Gong and defeated him, restoring balance to the world. This myth emphasizes the balance of elements and the importance of maintaining harmony between opposing forces.

- **Enforcer of Celestial Law**: Zhu Rong is also known for his role in maintaining the order of heaven. He is often depicted as a judge or enforcer who punishes those who defy the celestial laws. His association with fire underscores his role as a purifier and transformer, ensuring that justice is served and balance is maintained.

Additional Facts

- **Connection to the South**: Zhu Rong is associated with the direction South and the summer season. In the traditional Chinese cosmology of the Five Phases (Wu Xing), he represents the fire element, which corresponds to the South.

- **Historical Texts**: Zhu Rong is mentioned in several classical Chinese texts, including the "Classic of Mountains and Seas" (Shan Hai Jing) and the "Records of the Grand Historian" (Shiji) by Sima Qian, which provide insights into his role and significance in ancient mythology.

Resources

1. "Classic of Mountains and Seas" (Shan Hai Jing): An ancient Chinese text that includes descriptions of mythological figures, including Zhu Rong.

90

ZOMBIE (THE UNDEAD)

(HAITIAN)

Description

Zombies are mythological creatures often depicted as reanimated corpses brought back to life through supernatural means. Unlike their modern counterparts, which are typically portrayed as mindless, flesh-eating beings, traditional mythological zombies vary widely in appearance and behavior. These undead entities are often associated with curses, black magic, and voodoo practices.

Origin

The concept of zombies has ancient roots and appears in various cultures worldwide. The term "zombie" is believed to have originated from West African and Haitian folklore. In Haitian Vodou, a "zombi" refers to a corpse reanimated by a sorcerer, or "bokor." These zombies are typically under the control of the bokor and lack free will.

In addition to Haitian folklore, the idea of reanimated corpses can be found in ancient civilizations such as Mesopotamia, Egypt, and Greece. The Epic of Gilgamesh, one of the oldest known works of literature, mentions the dead rising to feast on the living. Similarly, the Egyptian Book of the Dead includes spells to protect the deceased from reanimation.

Lore

Zombie lore varies significantly across different cultures and time periods. Common themes include:

- **Reanimation**: Zombies are typically reanimated through magical or supernatural means, such as curses, spells, or the intervention of deities.
- **Control**: Traditional zombies often lack free will and are controlled by the person or entity that reanimated them. In Haitian Vodou, zombies are said to be used as laborers or for malevolent purposes by the bokor.

Additional Facts

- **Historical Accounts**: Historical records from Haiti describe individuals who were allegedly turned into zombies through the use of potent poisons and psychological manipulation. These accounts have contributed to the mystique surrounding zombies in Vodou culture.
- **Regional Variations**: Different cultures have unique versions of zombie myths. In Chinese folklore, "jiangshi" are reanimated corpses that hop towards their victims and suck their life force. In Scandinavian mythology, "draugr" are undead beings that guard their burial mounds and possess superhuman strength.

Resources

- "Zombies: A Cultural History" by Roger Luckhurst.

About the Author

Ethan Howard is the founder of *A Blind Guy's View*, a YouTube channel where he reviews movies, with a particular focus on classic films. In addition to his work as a content creator, Ethan is also the proud father of two beautiful children, Hadley and Holden. He has written several books in his "Epic" series and is set to release his upcoming novel, *Eppica's Lily*, in late 2024.

Growing up in southern Oregon, Ethan has spent over 15 years working for the U.S. Forest Service and has taught Geospatial Science at Oregon Tech for more than a decade. Diagnosed with Stargardt's Dystrophy at the age of 14, Ethan has never let his visual impairment hold him back, demonstrating a deep passion for storytelling, the outdoors, and education. He hopes his resilience and creativity continue to inspire those around him.

Contact Ethan directly at ABlindGuysView@gmail.com

Soli Deo gloria

Made in the USA
Monee, IL
18 October 2026

66036548R00109